Fernán Caballero

Elia or Spain fifty years ago

Fernán Caballero

Elia or Spain fifty years ago

ISBN/EAN: 9783741189869

Manufactured in Europe, USA, Canada, Australia, Japa

Cover: Foto ©ninafisch / pixelio.de

Manufactured and distributed by brebook publishing software (www.brebook.com)

Fernán Caballero

Elia or Spain fifty years ago

A WORD FROM THE AUTHOR TO THE READER.

You may not be indulgent, dear reader; and in truth, one who thrusts himself before the public, without being compelled to do so, has no right to exact indulgence.

It is the reader's province to be a judge; good or bad, a judge he is, and no one can depose him from his office. Indulgence is a favor, and to sue for it a politeness, which no author will omit who has read Lord Chesterfield.

And first, we desire to clear ourselves of certain charges which will be brought against us.

Balzac says, "We shall all die misunderstood. This is the death of women and authors." How true this is!

Those who consider the celebrated Heloise as the true type of a woman crossed in love, will perhaps look upon our Elia as insipid and false to nature, under similar circumstances; but we would remind them that the pure love of a girl, brought up in a convent and attached to it, is, in every respect, the opposite of that of the self-willed woman, who regards the convent in which she is immersed as a hateful prison that separates her from the man whom she elevates by her affection.

It may be that a woman who does not love to madness is not the ideal of the masses, but she is, we feel sure, of all those—less romantic but more poetical—who sympathize with truth and simplicity rather than with fiction and affectation.

This want of passion, when it proceeds from purity of soul, the force of reason, the influence of religion, and feminine delicacy, far from being despised by men, should be greatly appreciated by them, forming, as it does, that contrast to the masculine character which gives woman all her enchantment in man's eyes.

We may be charged with the want of reason of some of our personages in their arguments. To this we answer, all speak and argue according to their characters, and the author is in no wise responsible for them. We do not even maintain that the sayings and arguments of the Lady of Calatrava, who possesses all our sympathy, are entirely orthodox.

The spiritualism of such men as Doctor Narciso is an affectation and hypocrisy; but the spiritualism which elevates man above sensual passion and worldly pleasure is not the dream of a visionary of strong mind and feeble body—no. Spiritualism exists; but, even in literature, it exists, simple, natural, and stable, upon its firm and only basis, true religion.

The proof of this assertion is found in the portrait of Elia, painted from life, which we here present to the public.

Reader, you may find fault with the copy, but the *original* is far above criticism.

ELIA;

OR,

SPAIN FIFTY YEARS AGO.

CHAPTER I.

It was one of the loveliest of the many lovely days which the good God has bestowed, as an inheritance, upon the Catholic land of Spain. The sun's rays, falling to the earth in a flood of golden light, after copious showers, had bedecked Andalusia as with a garment woven of brilliants; while in the calm blue sky a few light, undefined clouds resembling lace of the finest texture, floated lazily hither and thither, impelled by a fickle zephyr as in a tranquil and poetic mind flit vague and fanciful conceptions. The air, redolent with the perfume of the orange-blossom, vibrated to the sound of bells and the powerful voice of cannon, announcing the solemnity of the day to the overjoyed inhabitants of the ever-faithful city of Seville. From all the balconies of the town gay streamers and bright banners were waving merrily to and fro, as if animated by the general gladness; and gayly-dressed persons of both sexes, with faces radiant with happiness, conversed and embraced in the public streets, and filled the air with shouts of joy and satisfaction, as they wended their way toward the grand cathedral, whose magnificent organ was sending up to heaven the ravishing music of the *Te Deum*. Oh, it was a profound, electrical, magnetic happiness which filled all hearts, moistened all eyes, and placed upon each lip a hymn of praise and thanksgiving to the Lord of hosts—the God of armies. Ferdinand the Seventh again occupied the throne of his ancestors!

After the *Te Deum*, the likeness of the legitimate and longed-for monarch was carried through the city, followed by the authorities and a brilliant military escort.

In one corner of the balcony of an ancient

house, seated in a low arm-chair, was an old lady, of a mild, benevolent aspect, shedding tears of happiness, and throwing flowers, with both hands, upon a body of hussars, who formed the advance-guard of the procession. She wore a black silk dress, a shawl of black thread lace, and a black mantilla thrown carelessly over her gray hairs, and displayed ostentatiously a necklace of large pearls, to which was attached a miniature of the sovereign set in diamonds. Behind this person, and supplying her with flowers from a basket which he held in his arms, stood a man of middle age and demure countenance, whose eyes sparkled with delight as they rested upon the triumphal car which bore the portrait of the king. At the opposite end of the balcony sat another lady, richly but simply dressed, whose beauty age had dimmed, but could never wholly mar.

Between the two, leaning against the railing of the balcony, was a young girl who had the distinguished and impassible beauty of a statue. The richness of her attire appeared to concern her as little as the admiration of which she was the object.

1*

"Who is that beautiful girl?" asked an artillery officer, a stranger to Seville, of one of his friends.

"Esperanza Orrea, daughter of the Marchioness of Val de Jara," was the reply.

"Do you know her?"

"Yes; we are related. Her great-grandmother was a third cousin of mine. Here we follow the trail of genealogy as a pointer follows a hare."

"Take me to her house, then," said the officer, "for Cupid has shot at me through her beautiful eyes."

"Now God forbid!" exclaimed his friend. "She and all her family are *conservatives*; and you, who incline to liberalism, would be received by her like a dog at mass."

"I will wait, then, until Carlos Orrea, who is as liberal as I, arrives. But tell me, the old lady whose face is so pitted with small-pox, does she belong to the same family?"

"That is Doña Isabel de Orrea, eldest sister of the Marquis of Val de Jara, and widow of the powerful and widely-celebrated Asistente *

---

* *Asistente* is the title of the chief magistrate of Seville.

of Seville, Don Manuel Farfan and Calatrava.
Her history is interesting, my mother has often
told me it. At seventeen, the lovely and only
daughter of the Marquis of Val de Jara, she was
about to be married to one whom she dearly
lovde· In one short year she lost her lover, who
was instantly killed by a fall from his horse, and
came near dying herself with the small-pox,
which disfigured her terribly ; and finally, her
father, by a second marriage, had a son, whose
birth deprived her of titles and estates. But
nothing could deprive her of her excellent and
amiable disposition. She attached herself to
her step-mother with sincere affection, and loved
her brothers (two in number) as if they had
been her own mother's children. The eldest
was father of the charming Esperanza, of your
friend Carlos, and of his brother Fernando; the
second, an officer of the navy, died at Trafalgar,
leaving an only daughter, who was brought up
by her aunt the Asistenta and is now the wife
of the Count of Palma, our ambassador at the
court of St. James. Isabel Orrea married the
Asistente late in life, and at his death fell heir
to the immense wealth left him by his father the
Viceroy of Mexico."

"And the marchioness?"

"Of the house of Cordoba, my friend, whose blood, as you know, is bluer than the indigo of the city of that name. There is no entrance into her palace, I can tell you! There plays are prohibited, balls anathematized, courtships banished, and gallantry forbidden fruit. Take my advice, then, and like the fox in the fable who found the grapes too high for him, content yourself with gazing at a distance on the object of your desire."

The officer cast a penetrating glance at his friend, and asked. "Is this the advice of a friend or a rival? Perhaps *you* are smitten with the fair damsel!"

"I?" exclaimed the other, bursting into a hearty laugh. "You deceive yourself greatly. I am not such a simpleton, believe me."

"And the man who looks like a clergyman?" said the artilleryman, returning to his questioning.

"Is Doctor Benigno, son of the steward of the deceased Asistente, who educated him for the church, but finding that he could not get beyond the first orders on account of his want of capacity, took him as his secretary, as he wrote a good hand, which place he continued to fill with the widow. He is a simple-hearted man, whose fidelity to his benefactress is his best eulogium."

After the procession had passed, the ladies of Calatrava and Orrea betook themselves to the residence of the former, who had prepared a great dinner for the occasion. The house was one of the grandest in Spain, the entrance to its court-yard being through an arched vestibule of massive stone, in the wings of which were the stable, carriage-house, and grooms' rooms. In the rear of the court-yard was a garden of some fifteen acres, where lofty cypresses and wide-spreading orange-trees attested its antiquity; and without being at all romantic or poetical, one could readily imagine, while looking at them, that they had lost the reckoning of the generations of lords which they had sheltered, and of the generations of men to whom they had given shade. The dinner, which was brought in on silver dishes, put to shame that of Camacho's wedding. At dessert the marchioness said: "Let us drink now to the extermination of all the enemies of the altar and the throne, those two holy and eternal foundation-stones of society!"

"No," replied the Asistenta; "on this happy day, I will think alone of restoration, not extermination. Let us drink, then, to the health of all the brave defenders of our country, and to the speedy return of your two gallant sons, sister."

CHAPTER II.

OPPOSITE to Seville, beyond Triana, there extends a vast plain, which seems to descend from the distant hills for the purpose of drinking in the waters of the Guadalquivir. Far to the left, the highlands themselves approach the river, depositing on its brink the little village of San Juan, crowned with a convent, erected upon the ruins of an immense Moorish castle, like a cross upon a turban. On the very summits of the hills are the villages of Tomares, Castilleja de la Cuesta, and Castilleja de Guzman, and, in the plain, Camas and Santi-Ponce, whose black flag is raised, like a cry of anguish, when the floods descend upon them, as a signal to Seville to open her granaries and send her children to the rescue. Near the last-mentioned village two young men, stretched at full length upon the grass, gazed wistfully upon the magnificent panorama before them. The elder of the two was clad in the simple uniform of a guardsman, while the younger wore with easy grace the gold-embroidered jacket and showy trappings of a hussar. His cap lay beside him on the ground, and the wind played with the ringlets of his raven hair.

"How glad I am, Fernando," said the latter, "to see the Geralda once more. This at least the French were not able to carry off with them. Robbers that they are! how we thrashed them at last! Thank God! we have peace once more; and yet, accustomed as I am to camp life, I fear I shall find it dull enough at home, and be compelled to resort to my old tricks for amusement. Do you remember the night when aunt came to our house in her antique carriage, drawn by the ancient mules, and driven by old John, and I cut the reins and traces? At length, you remember, aunt giving the order, John started up the mules and away they went, without once looking behind them. I can see John now, as he appeared with the reins in one hand and the uplifted whip in the other, and his mouth and eyes wide open, while aunt cried out: 'This is some of Carlos's deviltry, who diverts himself at his aunt's expense.—Wait till to-morrow, ingrate, and you will find yourself in the penitentiary!'"

"But, Carlos," said the grave guardsman, "remember you are no longer a child, and should respect as well as love our good aunt, who has been a second mother to us. Recollect, too, that you have but little patrimony, and that your future is in aunt's hands."

"Brother," answered Carlos, "I love and respect my aunt, because she is the best of aunts and the best of women; because, without a silly hair in her head, she has the frankness and simplicity of a child, with the heart of an angel. As to what she may leave me in her will, God forbid that I should ever think of it!"

"But your future?"

"Is not that of a millionnaire, I admit. Let me see—I am the owner of a house worth eight thousand dollars, which has a mortgage upon it of nine thousand; a plantation of olive-trees, which the French burned down; and a vineyard that gives vinegar. What then? '*Gold, you know, is a chimera,*' as the French sang while they were robbing us. And I have my sabre and I have you. What more could I desire?"

Fernando smiled with profound satisfaction. "You speak, Carlos," said he, "like my own dear brother and my best friend." At this moment a servant presented himself, with their horses, when, throwing themselves into the saddle, the brothers rode at full speed toward Seville. When they reached the house of their mother, they found the marchioness had gone to their aunt's, whither they betook themselves without delay.

Who can describe the joy of the whole household upon seeing the brothers—who had left home almost children—return safe and sound, with their breasts covered with crosses of honor, after a long and bloody war! The marchioness, pale as death, was speechless from emotion, the Asistenta wept aloud; Esperanza embraced them by turns at least a score of times; and Doctor Benigno, crossing his hands, raised his eyes to heaven and his heart to God. Carlos, wild with happiness, hugged everybody. "John," cried he to the old coachman, "I have not a razor to cut the reins of your mules, but look out for my sabre. It has a keen edge on it, I can tell you.—Maria," continued he, addressing himself to the housekeeper, "I have not lost my taste for sweet things. Take good care of your keys, and place a watchman over the pantry!"

"Aunt," said Fernando, "you will rejoice, I know, when I tell you Clara will shortly be here. Her health is somewhat delicate, and her physicians have advised her to pass the winter in Andalusia."

"God be thanked!" cried the Asistenta; "my cup of happiness is indeed full."

While Fernando was talking, Carlos was turning his head in every direction. "Aunt," said he, at length, "your house is like a clock that doesn't go. I see nothing new in it but the likeness of the long-nosed king."

"Long-nosed!" exclaimed the Asistenta. "How dare you speak thus of your sovereign?"

"By Jupiter!" replied Carlos, "cannot a king have a long nose as well as a plebeian? Must he necessarily—"

"He has *not* a long nose," interrupted the

Asistenta; "but if he had a trunk like an elephant, it would be irreverent in his subjects to notice it. I tell you that such a nickname applied to the king must have been invented by a rebel, and could be repeated by none but *liberals.*"

"Why, my dear aunt, you use the word *liberal* as if it meant a Frenchman or a thief. A liberal, I'd have you to know, is a game Spaniard, like myself."

"Ave Maria! An Orrea, a liberal and in league with the rabble!" cried the Asistenta. "Have you lost your senses, child?"

"With what have you been associating since you left your home?" said the marchioness, bitterly. "Have you been to Cadiz, the cradle of license, misnamed liberty?"

"He is mad," exclaimed the Asistenta.

"He is possessed, which is worse," said the marchioness.

"Great Heaven! what an explosion! My dearly-beloved conservatives, what do you suppose a liberal to be—a fellow who eats children raw—a Herod or a Robespierre?"

"If they are not all Robespierres," said

the marchioness, "they navigate in their waters."

"A liberal is one," chimed in the Asistenta, "who wishes to destroy the throne and level our altars to the dust."

"No, aunt, no. You are wrong, entirely wrong. A liberal is one who wishes Spain to awake, and not lie dreaming over past glory. True liberals recognize no other government than that of the king, no other than the Catholic faith."

"This is the gold with which the pill is gilded that, once swallowed, poisons the whole system," said the marchioness, vehemently. "I wonder, Fernando, that you listen so calmly to words that prove your brother false to his religion and his ancestors."

"Mother," answered Fernando, "I do not think brothers should quarrel about their politics; but Carlos certainly should remember it is a son's duty to respect the opinions of his mother."

"That is true," responded Carlos, "and I should have remembered, too, that intolerance is the vice of conservatives."

"It is not their vice," said the marchioness, "but their virtue. Error tolerates—truth condemns."

"And who is the competent judge?" asked Carlos.

"God in heaven, experience on earth," answered the marchioness.

"Sister," intervened the Asistenta, "what Carlos has just said throws a new light on the matter. Those who respect and love the altar and the throne, however much they may differ with us in other respects, are in the main of the same mind as ourselves.—So, my dear boy, if you will promise me never to call the king long-nosed again, we are friends. Between a liberal such as you, and a conservative like me, there is not a hair's difference."

"You are quite right, good aunt of mine: the only difference is, that while you are whispering, '*Stand still,*' I cannot for the life of me keep from shouting out, '*Go ahead!*'"

CHAPTER III.

The ancestral house of the Counts of Palma was prepared, and the aunts assembled there to welcome the countess.

"What a quantity of baggage Clara has sent before her!" said the Asistenta. "From the number of trunks and boxes, I should imagine she had left the shops of London and Paris entirely empty."

"The women of England and France," replied the marchioness, "think of nothing but fashion and finery; and I suppose Clara's physicians have sent her here, where she will be removed from that whirlpool of excitement, because she needs entire rest of body and mind."

"I feel anxious about her," rejoined the Asistenta, "for she was always as frail as a jasmine, and I don't like the treatment of her great doctor a bit. The idea of any one living on chicken-broth—it is absurd!"

"Fernando," added the marchioness, "says her doctor has not only a great reputation with his faculty, but is looked upon as a *savant*. He found him an insufferable pedant—one of those unbelievers who are politely termed philosophers—and the worst of it is, he is a Spaniard born."

"I can assure him of one thing," exclaimed the Asistenta, "that so sure as I hear him say one word against the king or the Catholic faith, I shall fall upon him as St. James fell upon the Moors!—And you, Ines?"

"I shall avoid all trouble by not permitting him to enter my doors."

At this instant a light travelling-carriage drove into the court-yard, and a moment afterward the countess entered, accompanied by Fernando and Carlos, who had gone out to meet her. She was a young woman of twenty-five, remarkably pretty and graceful, and elegantly dressed in the French fashion.

Warmly embracing her aunts, she cried out, in a voice trembling from emotion, "I see no change in either of you, my dear aunts; but Esperanza, who was a child when I left home, is now a beautiful woman. Yes, my darling, you are indeed beautiful," she added, folding Esperanza in her arms, "although I must say you are horribly *fagotée.*"

"She is what?" asked the Asistenta.

"Badly dressed, dear aunt."

"Badly dressed!" exclaimed the Asistenta, holding up both hands; "what in the world are you thinking about? A black bombazine dress, lace mantilla, open-work silk stockings, and white satin shoes. I really think you must have left your senses in England, Clara!"

"Her skirt is entirely too narrow," answered Clara; "and the idea of your showing your gray hairs as you do—what shocking taste! Just wait till I open my travelling-bag, and I'll show you the greatest love of a wig you ever laid your eyes on; I got it for you in Paris."

"Holy Virgin del Carme!" cried the Asistenta, "*I* wear a wig indeed! I should as soon think of taking lodgings in a mad-house."

"It will make you appear ten years younger, aunt."

"But I do not want to appear younger than I am, I tell you, and I won't be made a fool of in my old age; so we might as well drop the subject."

"A woman of talent has said," remarked the countess, "that a wig was not invented to make one look well, but to prevent one from looking ill, and therefore—"

"But I, who have no talent, say to you," interrupted the Asistenta, "that I am not willing at the end of life to deck myself out like a frivolous Frenchwoman, when I have always prided myself on being an Andalusian. Besides, I am on very good terms with my gray hairs, and I wouldn't put that hair of a corpse on my head for all the wealth that Pizarro took from Atahualpa."

"You have not told us yet any thing about your husband," said the marchioness; "how is he, and how does he like England?"

"The count rather likes England, I think," was Clara's reply. "He is in excellent health."

"Sister was not asking you about the count, but about Juan Maria, your husband," observed the Asistenta.

"And with this understanding, I replied to her," answered Clara.

"Do you mean to tell me that you call your husband 'count?'"

"Isn't he a count, then, dear aunt?"

"Just hear her!" said the Asistenta. "And you on good terms with him?"

Clara burst out laughing, and embraced her aunt, saying, "Aunt, it is the custom among women of fashion to call their husbands by their titles, if they have them; and if not, 'Mister.'"

"Well, we live and learn; and does this custom extend to parents, brothers, sisters, uncles, aunts, and cousins, as well? Must we, for example, in order to be fashionable, address you as 'madame the countess,' my dear?"

"Now God forbid! dear aunt," answered Clara hastily, at the same time kissing the Asistenta's hand.

"Ah, I understand it all now," rejoined the Asistenta, "the fashionable women of France see so little of their husbands that they treat them with great ceremony when they chance to fall in with them. A fine way of living, truly!"

"How ugly and antiquated all this furniture is!" said Clara, yawning. "This is certainly the mansion of misanthropy. Why, a steam-engine is necessary to move these arm-chairs; and as for those pictures, they are enough to give one the blues."

"Horrible!" cried the Asistenta. "Where in the world could you find handsomer furniture than this, or walls more magnificently adorned, covered as they are with pictures by Velasquez and Murillo, of such value that they are chained to the wall to prevent their being stolen?"

"All very well for a church," answered the countess, "but entirely out of place here. I shall make a complete transformation!"

"You are mistress of your own house, and can do as you please with it. As for me, I should regard it as almost a sacrilege to make the slightest change in it," said the Asistenta. "Clara, antiquity sets a seal of nobility upon families, houses, and furniture, which parvenus envy in reality while they affect to despise it. Some years hence, what you now place here will be old without being antique, without bearing the stamp of its epoch, and it may be that this weathercock that you call fashion will then adore what it now ridicules and throws aside."

Seeing that what she had said gave displeasure to her aunt, whom she tenderly loved, Clara changed the subject by asking: "What has become of Elia? Is she as handsome as she used to be?"

"Elia," answered the Asistenta, with visible satisfaction, "is more beautiful than ever! She has been for the past six years in a convent, because every one said I was spoiling her, and that she would never learn any thing at home."

"But you surely don't intend to keep her there forever?"

"Most assuredly not; for, although she is perfectly satisfied where she is, I desire to have her with me until I die, when she can return to the convent if she prefers it."

"You should have taken her out of there a year ago, and she would have been spared a year of dull monotony."

"Elia does not find the convent dull," said the marchioness. "On the contrary, it will cost her many tears to leave it."

"She ought to see something of the world,"

rejoined Clara. "To imprison youth and beauty is monstrous, aunt!"

"How I long to see her!" exclaimed Carlos. "Don't you remember how I used to torment her, and how you used to scold me for it, sister."

"Yes, indeed," said Esperanza, "and you deserve a real good thrashing for it, for you were a perfect plague of a boy. I hope your camp-life has effected a reformation, however."

"You will take her out of the convent, aunt, I am sure you will," continued Carlos, "and I promise you not to tease her a bit."

"Yes," replied the Asistenta, "and then I shall see gathered around me all that I love upon earth. We will bring her home once more, will we not, Ines?"

She addressed these last words to her sister-in-law, because she had become accustomed to rely upon her firm and lucid judgment, and never remained fully satisfied with her own opinions unless they met with the approval of the latter. The marchioness, who was evidently not pleased with the turn the conversation had taken, contented herself with replying: "You know that a maniac knows more in his own house than a wise man in another's."

Just as the Asistenta was about replying with her usual vivacity, the door opened, and a gentleman advanced in life limped into the room as if he were afflicted with the gout. He was tall and thin, and wore gold spectacles on his long, pointed nose.

"This is my intimate friend, Doctor Narciso Delgado, to whose skill I am indebted for my life," said Clara. "I beg that you will look upon him as a member of the family."

Doctor Delgado saluted with affected courtesy, and apologized for presenting himself in a travelling-dress.

"What a scarecrow!" whispered the Asistenta to her sister-in-law. "He looks as if he had been fed upon garter-snakes."

Doctor Benigno now came in and greeted Clara with warmth but with great deference.

"Who is the domine?" asked Delgado, casting a disdainful glance at the inelegant figure of the secretary.

"He is the son of—" Clara commenced to reply, when the Asistenta broke in with—

"Doctor Benigno Cordero, at your service;" and then she continued, in an affected tone of voice: "he is my intimate friend, and I beg that you will look upon him as a member of the family."

Benigno blushed like a child. He was one of those persons whom the world calls unfortunate because they have not great minds. But why should he have desired a great mind? Genius is a luxury—at times useful, at times hurtful. It is a torch or a consuming fire, according to the use which is made of it, and, as Lavergne says, "it is the inveterate enemy of the heart." And, in place of it, he possessed excellent common-sense, which, if not a sun, is at least a fixed star. He rarely asked advice; not because he despised the opinions of others, but because he was seldom or never in doubt as to the proper management of the estate which the Asistenta had intrusted to his care. If he sometimes lacked energy and determination, he performed every Christian duty with zeal and sincerity. He looked upon the evil passions of men as infirmities, and pitied those afflicted with them from the bottom of his soul; and, although his correct deportment gave him a right to be hard with transgressors, no word of censure was ever heard to fall from his lips.

He served his benefactress with the fidelity of a dog; and in saying this, it must be borne in mind that we know of nothing more touching or beautiful than this figure portrays.

CHAPTER IV.

On the following day the Asistenta, as was her custom, rose at seven o'clock and went to church. She heard two masses, seated in a low arm-chair, brought to her by one of the convent-boys, examined and carefully dusted an altar which she had taken under her especial charge, said her prayers to the Virgin, gave alms to the poor, and returned home with her heart light at the remembrance of good works done.

Breakfast was now served up to her, consisting of ham and eggs, hot cakes and chocolate, after partaking of which she withdrew to the library; where she found a budget of papers, letters, and notes, which Benigno immediately began to read to her. Among the notes was one from a lady announcing the death of a highly-esteemed man, who had left his widow in a despairing condition.

"I must go to the house of weeping immediately," said the good woman, and she was about rising from her seat, when Benigno stopped her, saying he had a letter from her lawyer in Madrid concerning a lawsuit in which she was engaged.

"I have no time to listen to it," replied the Asistenta; "I must go to the poor widow."

"Señora," exclaimed Benigno, with a look of alarm, as he cast his eyes over the letter, "we have lost the lawsuit!"

"Did you not hear me say I had no time to listen to you?" asked the Asistenta, springing to her feet, and beginning to put on her mantilla.

"But," continued the afflicted secretary, "your solicitor says you should appeal to a higher court."

"I shall do no such thing," replied the señora calmly.

"And why not, your excellency?"

"In the first place, because I detest lawsuits, and am glad this one is over, although it has gone against me; and, secondly, I have learned that the plaintiff is in needy circumstances. So we will leave things as God has fixed them."

"Condemned to pay the costs, too!" groaned Benigno. "How can this be done, how can this be done?"

"By selling oil and corn, and then putting your hands in your pockets and taking out the money."

"Sell to raise money!" cried Benigno, scandalized at the suggestion (for he was an excellent administrator and economist), "you mistake my meaning, señora, we have money enough and to spare, and prices are low; but the costs are out of all reason. Look at this charge, for instance."

"I repeat, I have not time—I must go to the widow."

"Here is a letter asking alms."

The Asistenta turned round and seated herself; but Benigno, whose whole soul was in the bill of costs, did not observe her until she asked for the letter.

"Pardon me, your excellency," said he, "I thought you had not time to listen to it."

"And what excuse could I offer to His Divine Majesty for denying myself to the poor?' said the good woman.

Doctor Benigno opened the letter and read:

"SEÑORA:

"An unhappy woman, lying on a mat, has recourse to your worship, whose charity is so well known. I am as helpless and naked as I was when I came into the world. I beseech you, then, to give me the means of covering my flesh, in order that, in the hour of my approaching death, my guardian angel may not turn his back upon my nakedness. By this act of charity you will prepare a swaddling-band for the infant Jesus next Christmas, who will not fail to give you your reward in this world and the next."

The Asistenta called Maria. "You must go at once to see this afflicted woman," said she, "and Doctor Benigno will send our family physician to her, and desire the apothecary to supply her with medicine at my expense.—Now that I think of it, was the apothecary's bill large last month?"

"No, señora," replied the secretary, "only a hundred dollars."

"I am thankful the health of the city continues good, and now I must be off—my mantilla, Maria."

Before proceeding further in our story, we have two words to say about this good servant.

Maria was a woman of fifty-six years, very neat in her person, and a most excellent and careful housekeeper, but an inveterate fault-finder and grumbler. She entered the Asistenta's service as a girl; and after living with her some years, married a schoolmaster, by whom she had two sons, who, with their father and an infant only six weeks old, all died in the year of the great epidemic; and as it so happened that the Asistenta was just then looking for a wet-nurse for Elia, Maria was employed in this capacity, and afterward retained as housekeeper. She was, to use a vulgar expression, the hands and feet of her mistress, who gave her a *carte blanche* to do as she pleased, and resigned to her and the steward Pedro the entire charge of her household. For Maria there were neither locks nor secrets. She placed her spoon in every thing, and for the most part with judgment and discretion. Her mistress had declared to her, on the previous evening, her intention of removing Elia from the convent, and the good woman was in ecstasies at the announcement.

As the Asistenta was going down the great staircase leading to the court-yard, she met the marchioness coming up.

"What good thought brought you hither at this hour, sister?" asked the former, affectionately.

"I wish to speak to you in private, Isabel."

As the Asistenta led the way to a sofa in the library, Don Benigno, after respectfully saluting the marchioness, retired, followed by Maria, who took herself off with a very bad grace. "A visit at this hour," she grumbled to herself, "cannot be for any good purpose; I lay my life the marchioness has come here to give advice where it is not needed. She never did like Elia, and would gladly place another bar across the door of the convent which holds the poor child."

"Yesterday, Isabel," began the marchioness,

"you desired me to give you my opinion in relation to Elia."

"Yes," responded the Asistenta, with some warmth, "and I have not forgotten your ungracious reply, Ines!"

"It was not a proper time or place to speak deliberately and freely on a grave matter," rejoined the marchioness; "but before proceeding further, let me ask you how you intend to place Elia?"

"By my side, Ines."

"But upon what footing?"

"As my daughter."

"Are you sure the world will concede to her this position?"

"Who can object, if I grant it to her?"

"Those who know it is not in your power, not even in the power of God Himself, to annul the past—those who know that nobility does not admit grafts on its illustrious trunk, which only deigns to nourish its legitimate branches."

"Gracious Heaven, Ines!" exclaimed the Asistenta, "is it necessary, in order to love and appreciate this angelic child, that we should inquire after her patents of nobility? Would you ask the rose, before deigning to partake of its fragrance, whether it was brought up in a porcelain vase or a potter's vessel?"

"I do not see any similarity between persons in society and flowers in a flower-pot," replied the marchioness, coldly. "It is necessary to treat grave matters gravely. It will not do to leave the future, like a weathercock, to every chance wind that blows. True affection is not blind; it is far-seeing. What happiness can you offer to this child, in society, which will be at all comparable to that which she now enjoys in the convent?"

"None."

"What induces you to bring her here, then?"

"The love I bear her."

"It is not true love, Isabel."

"Those only understand love who feel it, Ines!"

"But what advantage will accrue to either of you from this change?"

"To her, a knowledge of the world as well as of convent-life, so that when she chooses her lot she will know what she renounces; to me, the joy of having my darling with me to cheer my last hours, as the nightingale enlivens the declining day. When I am dead, she can return to the convent if she elects to do so."

"It may then be too late, sister."

"I trust the future to God's hands, Ines."

"Promise me at least, sister, to take more time to ponder this matter."

"Ines," cried the Asistenta, impetuously, "he who walks in the street of *To-morrow* will bring up in the square of *Never!*"

"Very well, then, Isabel," said the marchioness rising and walking slowly toward the door· "since you reject my advice, I can only beg you to remember that I have given it to you, and pray to God that you may never have cause to repent not having taken it."

The marchioness had scarcely left the room when Maria entered it, with her face converted into a note of interrogation.

"Put your shawl on," said her mistress, "and, after calling to see the sick woman, go to the convent and say to the lady-abbess, with my warmest love, that three days hence I shall send for my darling to live with me, during the remainder of my days. And now I must away to the widow's, even if the bishop himself should be announced." Saying this, she departed, leaving Maria with a glad heart.

"The marchioness might as well have stayed at home, with her worldly *pruderies* and proud *categories*," soliloquized she. "They soon dash themselves to pieces against the firm goodness of heart of the señora."

CHAPTER V.

THREE days had passed, and the Asistenta was seated in her bedroom, listening to Don Benigno reading the "Christian Year." "Lay the 'Christian Year' aside," said the señora, who seemed to have the *fidgets*, "and read something from 'Don Quixote.'"

Don Benigno obeyed, casting a wistful glance at Father Crasser's work as he put it down, for his quiet and devout nature sympathized rather with the friar than with the witty Cervantes, especially as he felt greatly shocked and grieved at finding a knight of such excellent intentions, in almost all his wanderings so roughly handled. But he had scarcely read five lines when the Asistenta interrupted him anew with "No more, no more, Don Benigno. Dorothea is stupid, and your reading so monotonous to-day that I seem to be listening to a monk's chanting. What time is it?"

"A quarter of two," replied the reader, lugging out a silver watch large enough for a clock, and as round as a turnip.

"How they do make me wait!" exclaimed the Asistenta; "and as for that Maria, when she once commences chattering, she never knows how to stop."

"As the sisters love the child so dearly, their leave-taking will naturally be long and tender," said Don Benigno.

"And my nieces and nephews will get here before her," continued the Asistenta. "Ines was the only one who did not speak of coming to meet her; but she cannot and will not dissemble the anger she feels at my bringing the child home; and this takes away somewhat from my own pleasure. It is not kind in Ines."

"Señora," answered the secretary, "I have not observed this, and it seems to me impossible that the marchioness can be displeased with any thing you do."

"I do not wonder at your not observing it," cried the Asistenta, impatiently; "for I really believe a donkey might fly through the air without its attracting your notice; and as for excuses, you are capable of making one for the treachery of Judas.—Gracious! there goes the cathedral clock striking two!"

"Goodness me, señora!" said Maria, who entering at this instant, overheard her, "the convent is not within a stone's throw, I can tell you. It is a good journey there and back."

"Child of my heart," exclaimed the Asistenta, as Elia ran and threw herself into her arms, "how glad I am to see you! But you are weeping, dearest; don't you wish to remain with me?"

"Indeed I do, my dear mother. I never will leave you again; but I can often go to see the sisters, can I not?"

"Whenever you wish, my darling; so dry your tears, for when I see others crying, I cry too, and then my head aches." As the Asistenta spoke, she pressed the child to her bosom, and covered her head and face with kisses.

Elia was of medium size and perfectly formed. Her large black eyes, had they not worn so sweet an expression, would have seemed out of all proportion to her charming face, wherein the rose and the olive strove for mastery; but her greatest attraction consisted in the mixture of sprightliness and simplicity which was observable in all she said and did. She wore a jacket of black serge, a skirt of the same, plaited at the waist, and morocco shoes with large silver buckles, and had a white muslin handkerchief around her neck tied in a bow under her chin. Her hair was parted in the middle, and hung in tresses down her back, reaching nearly to the ground.

While the Asistenta was caressing her, the door opened, and in came the countess, Fernando, Carlos, and Doctor Narciso; and as Elia looked toward them, all were struck with her surpassing beauty. Clara embraced her repeatedly, and, looking at her from head to foot, exclaimed: "You must be as beautiful as Venus, you little witch you, to look as you do in that outlandish garb! Do you remember me, Elia?"

"Certainly, Clara; I remember you perfectly well, and that you are now the Countess of Palma. I have not forgotten, either, your kindness to the poor orphan, nor your giving me that beautiful bracelet when you went away—and the white rats—alas! poor little things, they died long ago."

"And do you remember me, Elia?" said Carlos.

"Carlos!" exclaimed Elia, and a radiant smile mingled with the tears which were yet running down her cheeks. "Did you suppose that your lace and whiskers had so disguised you that I would not know you? They are more becoming than your student's dress which you used to be so fond of tearing."

"You have not entirely forgotten me, I hope," said Fernando, in a somewhat formal manner.

The color mounted into the child's cheeks as she replied. "No, señor; in the convent no one is forgotten, nothing changes."

"And do you suppose," cried Carlos, warmly, "that in the world one forgets the ties of love and friendship? You would not think so if you only knew how often I thought of you when the balls were flying about me, and I said to myself, 'This is not so pleasant as when Elia and I threw acorns at each other;' and then—"

"Come, come, Mister Hussar," interrupted

Clara, "you are expending rather too much gallantry on a little nun. Wait, at least, until she is dressed like a rational being, before uttering any more of your high-flown nonsense.—Aunt," she continued, turning toward the Asistenta, "I will take Elia with me, and bring her back to your reception to-night, dressed as she ought to be, for she is a perfect caricature now."

"This shall be attended to, to-morrow."

"No, no, this very day, aunt; she is unpresentable as she is. Please don't deprive me of this pleasure; for Heaven knows there are few enough in this antediluvian Seville!"

"Let me stay with my mother to-day," said Elia; "for I have so much to tell her and so many presents to give her from the nuns." As she said these last words, Doctor Delgado smiled sarcastically, and quoted the ill-natured saying: "Give a bushel of wheat to a nun, and she will make you a biscuit."

"So say the sons of the devil," cried the Asistenta, "when they see the rich giving of their abundance to the poor nuns!"

"Poor nuns!" echoed the doctor. "Say rather egotistical beings who separate themselves from the world, either through caprice or laziness, and hold their heads very high because, as they presume, they are reserving for God hearts incapable of feeling love or inspiring it."

Elia, astounded at these words, turned her face instinctively from this bitter man and hid it in the lap of her mother.

"Señor, señor," exclaimed the latter, "you talk of convents as I suppose a blind man would talk of colors. Let me tell you, then, what I have seen there—matrons of eighty years with the simplicity of children, seraphs of twenty unmindful of their youth and beauty, and a serenity of soul with both unknown to the world, and—"

"Aunt," said Clara, interrupting her, "I am off with Elia. We are of the same height, and after my maid has put one of my dresses on her and arranged her hair, you won't know her. Come along, Elia." So saying, she seized Elia by the hand and ran off with her, and in a few minutes her carriage was heard driving rapidly away.

"There is no denying that witch any thing,"

said the Asistenta; "I don't wonder that Juan Maria would not take no f.r an answer, as she boasts so often."

At the evening reception all amused themselves as their inclinations prompted. The marchioness and the Asistenta, with a few others, played cards; while a number of ladies seated themselves around a large *brasero* and chatted pleasantly together, as they sipped their chocolate, for which Maria was so famous.

"And so," said the Baroness de Bruno, "this child is back again, is she? What in the world can have induced the Asistenta to remove her from the convent?"

"It is not hard to guess, I should say," replied Doña Marianita, an old maid of the Orrea family, whom every one loved for her amiability. "The pleasure of having her by her side to cheer her old age. In every thing Isabel acts like a mother toward a darling child."

"So it is acting like a mother," retorted the baroness, "to bring up a foundling as if she were a lady, and, after filling her head with nonsense, marry her to a lackey!"

"I do not see why she should marry a

lackey," replied Doña Marianita, a little warmly. "She is well-bred, remarkably pretty, and will be rich; for, you may rely upon it, Isabel will leave her a handsome fortune."

"And do you suppose," returned the baroness, "that money will induce, I will not say a gentleman, but any man of respectability, to marry her?"

"Who knows but her parents are noble?" chimed in the wife of General Rios. "Have you never been able to learn any thing about her, Marianita?"

"Not one word; all upon this subject have maintained a profound silence. During the great epidemic, Isabel went into the country, and on her return brought Elia with her. This is all I know. Maria, who nursed the child and adores her, is a closed chest; Pedro, the steward, a padlock; Juan, the coachman, deaf; Don Benigno, of course, dumb; and Isabel, who is open-mouthed about every thing else, said to me one day, when I questioned her about the child, that she was the daughter of the Grand Turk, and, seeing my astonishment, added, 'Marianita, ask me no questions, and I'll tell you no lies!'"

"If it be certain, as every one says," remarked the baroness, "that Isabel has kept but one secret in her life, it is equally certain that she has kept that one well!"

"It may be," said the general's wife, "that as Elia's birth took place during that fearful epidemic, both her parents died at the same time, and confided her to the Asistenta's care."

"It may well be so," replied Doña Marianita, "because she has told the child that she is the daughter of a very dear friend of hers, who died in giving her birth."

"Why this mystery, then?" asked the baroness, sourly.

"It is incomprehensible to me," replied Marianita, "but you may depend upon it, Isabella has good reasons for it."

"Don't deceive yourself," said the baroness; "there is no *good* reason for this secrecy. Something is wrong, and time will show it."

At this instant the countess entered, leading Elia by the hand. The young girl was beautifully attired in a white crape dress, looped up with roses, and wore a wreath of white japonicas upon her head. It was impossible to imagine an apparition more ideally beautiful. Without heeding any one, she ran to the Asistenta, and with a smile of infantile happiness, exclaimed, "Look, mother, how lovely I am!"

"As an angel of heaven," cried the Asistenta, folding her to her bosom.

All ran to greet her.

"She has been crowned with flowers," said Doctor Delgado, "to celebrate her emancipation from the convent."

Elia stood for a moment, as if bewildered; and then seizing the wreath which had given her so much pleasure, she threw it from her, exclaiming, "If there be any who think thus, I will not wear it."

CHAPTER VI.

When the Countess of Palma had arranged and transformed her house to suit the modern taste, assisted by the wise counsel of the elegant Narciso, she gave a large dinner-party, for the double purpose of surprising her family and friends, and of entertaining certain foreigners who had brought letters of introduction from her husband.

The marchioness could not be present, owing to a slight indisposition; and so her daughter remained at home with her, while Elia excused herself, and obtained permission to pass the day at the convent.

About ten o'clock at night, the two former were seated over a magnificent *brasero* of mahogany, inlaid with brass, when they heard a carriage drive rapidly up to the door. "Who can that be?" said the marchioness—"can it be your aunt?"

"When did her Methuselahs ever travel at that rate?" replied Esperanza, smiling.

She had scarcely got the words out of her mouth, however, when the door was thrown violently open, and in walked the Asistenta, followed by Don Benigno. "Sister! aunt!" cried mother and daughter in a breath. But the Asistenta, without noticing them, threw herself on a sofa, and began to fan herself so violently, that she broke her fan. "How out of breath you are, Isabel!" said the marchioness; "what has happened to you?"

"Before I say a word, Ines, let me have a cup of chocolate and a bit of bread. Such a dinner! and I, with the weight of eighty years on my shoulders, to be compelled to conform to French manners and customs!"

When the servants had brought in chocolate and biscuits, the Asistenta, somewhat composed, discoursed as follows:

"I could not have slept, sister, had I not first come here to tell you how topsy-turvy I found every thing in Clara's house. To realize it fully, however, you must see it for yourself. It appears really as if the world had a brain-fever. Change,

change, is the order of the day. Oh, how I do hate all innovators—beginning with the toadies and hangers-on at the court, and ending with this simpleton Delgado! But to the point. I went to Clara's at two o'clock. Imagine my astonishment, when, upon entering the court-yard, I missed the old fountain with its immense basin filled with gold-fish, and the statue of the knight in armor which we used to admire so much. 'Oh, Clara,' said I, 'how could you remove that antique statue, which always appeared an integral part of the house?'—'Dear aunt,' was her reply, 'people of taste say it was badly executed, and out of all proportion. It can only be put at the end of an avenue of trees, to heighten the perspective.'

"'And the box which you have taken away, what fault had you to find with it? Do you not know,' said I, 'that, among plants, it is the emblem of aristocracy, and is neither found wild, nor in the gardens of the lower classes; so that, on beholding it, we almost feel inclined to question it about our ancestors, and confide to it messages of love for our great-grandchildren?'—'But remember, aunt, it was in those hideous clay vases,' said Clara, 'and had been trimmed and retrimmed by the gardener's shears until it had lost all beauty in my eyes.' What could I reply to such nonsense, Ines?—But let us proceed. You will scarcely credit me, when I tell you that she has removed from the hall that magnificent collection of family portraits, and replaced them with pictures of famous men, as she calls them, in mahogany frames. I examined them carefully, Ines, and there is not one Spaniard among them. At the farther end of the hall, in the place of her uncle the cardinal, there is an old man with a face like a wolf's. Seeing me look at it very earnestly, the learned Narciso remarked that it was 'the likeness of the incomparable Voltaire.' 'Voltaire!' I exclaimed, 'that monster of wickedness, whose works are prohibited! Well, señor, it may truly be said of him that his face is as vile as his acts!' I entered the drawing-room, and lo and behold! the superb paintings of Murillo, Velasquez, and Carho have given place to engravings that are positively indecent. Among them is a representation of a shepherd embracing a goddess, as they call her, which is not fit to be put in a stable. 'Is it possible, Clara,' said I, 'that you can hang in plain view such a disgusting picture?'

"'The ideal elevates itself above the sensual,' said Don Narciso, stupidly and sententiously.

"'Señor,' I replied, 'prate as you please about your *ideal*, but here we call wine wine, and water water, and a naked woman is considered indecent.—Clara, Clara, if the Inquisition existed now, you would be forced to burn these prints.'

"'Inquisition!' exclaimed Narciso, giving a spring backward, and covering his face with his hands; 'señora, this word burns the mouth that utters it, and the ears that hear its mournful sound!'

"'Ah, señor,' I replied, 'if your conscience were as clear as mine, neither the word nor the institution itself would alarm you!'

"Clara insisted upon taking me to see the *improvements* she had made in the garden, and I did my best to try and admire them, for I saw she was mortified at what I had said; but, sister, it was impossible. She has removed the rock from the fountain; and as for the negro, mounted on a crocodile, with a plate of pineapples in his hand, I believe he has gone to Guinea to visit his kinsmen—the snakes; the lizards and the turtles have all gone, with the sea-shells which had been collected for generations. The paved walks have given place to clay paths, so that in rainy weather there will be no walking in it. It makes one indignant to see such devastation. Does it not, Don Benigno?"

Don Benigno made no reply. "Caspita!" exclaimed the Asistenta, impatiently; "a twenty-four pounder would not arouse this holy man from his torpor!"

"Señora," said the secretary, "it would not become me to censure the acts of your niece."

"He is right, as he usually is," said the marchioness.

"He is not right," replied the Asistenta, quickly. "Every man has a tongue in his mouth to censure what deserves censure, and Clara is not an exempt because she happens to belong to our family. But let me go on with my curious narration. It was now about three o'clock.—'When shall we dine, Clara?' 'At five,' was her reply. 'San Antonio!' I exclaimed—'and my siesta?'

"Clara directed her maid to bring me a cup of broth, and went off to dress, while I threw myself on a bed, to see if I could not at least catch a *canoniga*.* At five Clara came for me, and we went to the drawing-room, where I found, among other foreigners, a dapper little Frenchman, to whom Narciso was most obsequious. 'I'll bet ten to one, Clara,' said I, 'that they are abusing Spain.' At this moment the captain-general offered me his hand, to conduct me to the dining-room, and I asked him the Frenchman's name. 'Monsieur Maillard, the great violinist,' he replied, 'who is about to give a grand concert in the theatre of San Fernando.' 'Well done, well done!' said I. 'From a nobleman's house to the stage, eh? I, for one, will not go to hear him; for I know he'll play the *Marseillaise* or something akin to it.'—But now for the dinner, sister. Observing that our favorite dish was not on the table, I said to Clara, 'Your cook has forgotten the

* A nap before dinner is called a *canoniga* or *canon*, an after-dinner nap a *siesta*.

olla.'—'No, aunt,' she replied, laughing; 'I never eat it.'

"And then I overheard Narciso say to the violinist: 'A country of routine, my dear sir. Since the day when the first Spaniard ate *olla*, no one has been able to do without it.' There were many dishes, Ines, but all cooked with lard; so I waited for the second course, when what should I see, in the place of turkey and ham, but a haunch of venison? 'Clara,' said I, 'do you not know that none but the poorest people eat venison?'

"'Señora,' she replied, in a stately manner, 'venison is the favorite dish in London and Paris.'—'For the very good reason,' I rejoined, 'that in London and Paris it has a much more delicate flavor than in this country. Here it is rancid and flabby.'

"The pheasants were spoiled, and absolutely smelt badly; but Narciso declared that in this consisted their principal merit. 'When will the turkey make its appearance?' I asked.—'I never have turkey on my table,' was the reply, 'it looks so countryfied.' The dessert was abominable—none of our rich preserves or confectionery, but all sorts of stale *bon-bons* and candied fruits from Paris. I would not have tasted them for Paris itself. 'I never eat Spanish preserves,' said Narcisco, 'for they have too much sugar in them.'—'And would you have them preserved in salt?' said I. In fine, not to tire you to death, Ines, when the dinner was over, and I found the servants handing around tea instead of chocolate, I beat a hasty retreat and came here; and now I must be off, for John will be catching his death of cold on the coach-box, and I shall have eyes like a craw-fish's to-morrow. Remember, when you give a fashionable dinner party, you must have spoiled pheasant on your table, and preserves without sugar; and don't offend your guests by the slightest allusion to so vulgar a thing as a turkey—*a countryfied turkey*—ha, ha, ha! Good-night."

CHAPTER VII.

"You are making more flowers than the Spring, Elia," said Maria, one day, on finding her darling seated at a table covered with roses, jessamine, and violets. "The garden itself might envy you."

"I am not only making flowers," answered Elia, "but I am making verses also."

"Verses!" exclaimed the astonished housekeeper; "who taught you to make verses?"

"No one. I made them after Trisagio's, by counting the lines and imitating the rhymes, and have succeeded admirably, I can tell you—I was so anxious to succeed!"

"And what are they for?"

"For to-morrow, my mother's birthday. I have made this little basket of silver wire, to present to her too."

"That is right, my child," said Maria, "but

I have a great deal to do; so I must take myself off."

On the following day all the happy inmates of the house rose at an early hour, and with smiling countenances betook themselves in a body to the Asistenta's chamber, Don Benigno presenting her with a cake, about the size of a grindstone, adorned with flowers, among which was an immense rose, with a paper butterfly on it; and the servants chickens, ducks, turkeys, rabbits, fruits, and preserves.

Shortly after breakfast the relatives thronged the house, bringing with them all sorts of costly presents; and Don Narciso, who accompanied the countess, begged leave to read an ode which he had composed for the occasion. After fatiguing the ears of his hearers (the countess excepted) for an hour or more, he concluded; it being the infallible and fortunate law of compensations, that every thing on earth must come to an end sooner or later.

"But where is Elia?" asked Carlos.

"I don't know," replied the Asistenta. "Go and look for her, Carlos."

Carlos waited for no second bidding, but

hurried out of the room, and soon returned with Elia, carrying her little basket of flowers in her hand. Maria followed her with a grand air. But at sight of so many persons, and the beautiful presents spread on the table, Elia seemed bewildered, and stood still.

"My child," said the Asistenta, "why do you not run to me? Is that present for me?"

But Elia remained immovable.

"Come, come," cried Maria, "why do you not present your offering? Is it because you observe others more costly? One gives what one can afford to give, my darling."

"Maria is right," said the Asistenta, "and I shall value your gift, not for its costliness, but for the love I bear the giver."

"Go, my child," urged Maria, giving her a slight push with her elbow, without its being observed by the company, "your mother is waiting for you;" and then observing that Elia was about giving the basket without speaking, she could contain herself no longer, but cried out, "Not in that way, child, not in that way; but as you intended—reciting your verses, which must be good, since they were made after Trisagio's."

"Verses!" shouted all. The countess burst into a hearty laugh, and Doctor Narciso smiled satirically.

"Maria," said the mortified Elia, "this was a matter between us two; and just see how ridiculous you have made me!"

"A discreet enemy is better than a foolish friend, as the proverb has it," said Benigno in a low tone of voice to Maria.

"Ridiculous!" cried the Asistenta at the same time, in reply to Elia, "by no means, dearest. That which is prompted by affection can never be made to appear so. Come, my darling," she continued, coaxingly, "let me hear your verses; I warrant they will give me great pleasure."

Elia leaned her head on the Asistenta's shoulder, and, with her eyes cast down and filled with tears, recited in a low, tremulous voice as follows:

> "When as a babe, unconscious still,
> I lost my mother's care,
> You came her loving place to fill,
> And all my heart to share.

"And if a sinner's prayer to-day
 Is heard by God above,
 He will in favor you repay
 For all your deeds of love.

"His mercy will your life surround,
 And blessings send in showers,
 Just as I now bestrew the ground,
 Before you, with these flowers."

As she repeated the last words, she emptied her basket at the Asistenta's feet, who, leaning forward and clasping her to her bosom, exclaimed, "They are as simple and sweet as yourself, my angel!"

"And now," said the exultant Maria to Don Benigno, "what have you to say of the foolish friend, I should like to know?" and then turning to Doctor Narciso, she asked, "Can you deny, after this, sir, that good verses may be made by imitating Trisagio?"

"Certainly not," replied the doctor; "and it is a thousand pities that Boileau should have forgotten to mention this new method in his art of writing poetry."

"And cannot one write poetry without the

permission of Señor Bolo, I should like to know?" asked the housekeeper.

"Talk of soap-suds and corn-cakes, my good woman," responded Narciso, haughtily, "and don't make a fool of yourself about poetry!"

"Was there ever such an arrogant donkey?" murmured Maria to herself, half aloud. "He looks like a vinegar-cruet, and contains as much acid—I can't bear him."

The impressions caused by the scene between the Asistenta and Elia were various. The marchioness feared lest the exaggerated praise bestowed upon Elia should turn her head, and make a vain, worldly girl out of the pure, artless child of the convent.

Fernando, while he sympathized with his aunt, began to observe, with serious anxiety, the marked impression which the fair enchantress was producing upon the impassioned character of his brother; while the countess, as may be supposed, became so enthusiastic over the "verses" that she insisted upon the doctor's gathering "the beautiful wild flowers," as she called them, and inscribing them, "after being cultivated to suit his own refined taste," in her album.

But the doctor refused to attempt the task, affectedly declaring "that their leaves would be withered by his rude touch."

"And he speaks the truth," whispered Carlos to Elia; "for your verses are better than his ponderous ode, which seems to have had for its model, not the rhymes of Trisagio, but the long, stiff, and withered structure of its author."

But the one who was most astounded by all this, and who stood with his head bowed down before Maria, was Don Benigno, to whom a journey to Parnassus seemed as wonderful as the voyage of Columbus to the New World; and, as his modesty would not permit of his joining in the conversation of his superiors, he resolved, within himself, to repair to the convent on the morrow, and unburden his mind on the subject, not only to the abbess, but to the whole community.

"And now run and get your breakfast, Elia," said the Asistenta, "for you know you fasted all day yesterday."

"I did not know that one of your age was obliged to fast, Elia," remarked Delgado, in his bitter, satirical way.

"I am not obliged to," Elia replied, "but I fasted from devotion and choice."

"And do you think that to keep the stomach empty is a mark of devotion?"

"I do."

"And in what does it consist, my dear little girl?" asked the doctor, ironically.

"It consists in making a sacrifice."

"But of what benefit is this to God—can He derive either pleasure or advantage from an empty stomach?"

"God cannot derive advantage from any act of ours," answered Elia, "and therefore His Divine Majesty accepts the offering of our hearts and good intentions—which are all we have to bestow on Him."

"And it is no small matter, I can tell you," exclaimed Maria, "to bridle one's appetites, and oppose moderation to gluttony."

But Delgado, without deigning to notice her, continued: "Believe me, my child, true piety consists in being thankful for, and enjoying the goods which God has bestowed upon us. Let us lend a helping hand to suffering humanity, bend a knee before the Divine Creator—"

"And why not two?" interrupted the Asistenta. "Elia," she continued, "forgot to tell you, sir, who have learned in England to define your duties as a Christian, that fasting is a *precept*, whose merit consequently consists in the *submission* which obeys, the *humility* which does not question, the *deference* which respects, and the *self-denial* which carries out the commandment; as also in the public testimony of faith in the infallibility of the Church, which so wisely and for such holy ends orders all things. Señor Delgado," she added, slowly and impressively, "you are in a Catholic land, in a Catholic house, and in the presence of—praised be the Virgin!—a Catholic lady; and since you don't seem to know that your language is anti-Catholic, and offensive to the country, the house, and myself, it becomes my duty to remind you of the fact."

CHAPTER VIII.

So soon as the Asistenta's birthday had passed, she commenced making preparations to visit one of her country-seats near the city, and invited Fernando, Carlos, Clara, and Delgado to accompany her, all of whom accepted the invitation. As to Elia, she was mad with joy at the prospect of going into the country, which she called a "great garden," as she had called the convent "a little city."

At the time appointed, they set off in high spirits; the Asistenta and Elia in an old travelling-carriage, drawn by four vigorous mules (the *Methuselahs*, as Esperanza called them, having received a holiday on this occasion). Fernando and Carlos, dressed *à la* Andalusian—mounted on two superb colts, which had just been presented to them by their aunt, and Clara, with her doctor, in a light phaeton, drawn by two fast-trotting "bob-tails," which she had procured in England. On one side of the carriage rode Pedro, and on the other the overseer, armed with muskets.

They were received at the country-house, which was on the outskirts of a village, by the curate, and a crowd of farm-hands, while a troop of children, of all ages and of both sexes, surrounded the equipages, which they seemed to admire exceedingly, especially that of the countess. At length a cry arose, at first almost a whisper, but growing stronger, by the accession of one little voice after another, until it became almost a roar, of—"Horses without tails! horses without tails!" Upon hearing this explosion of surprise and astonishment, Clara and Carlos burst out laughing; not so the amiable Narciso, who raised his cane, and, threatening the little ones with it, cried out, angrily: "You should be silent, you little ragamuffins you, and respect even the horses of your betters!"

The youngsters dispersed like a flock of sparrows, but, with the temerity of these birds, returned immediately, and, encouraged by the smiles of the countess, shouted, pointing their fingers at Narciso, who happened to wear a small gray jockey-cap. "Behold old uncle with his brown-paper hunting-cap! How much will you take for it, uncle? I'll give you a penny!"

The doctor, finding the game decidedly against him, rushed into the house and slammed the door behind him, murmuring between his teeth—"Bedlamites! Hottentots! Savages!" But the nickname clung to him in the village, in which the elegant and distinguished guest of the first houses of England and France was always remembered as "old uncle with the brown-paper hunting-cap." Truly, "no one is a prophet in his own country."

The whole party now seemed bent on enjoyment. Their days, which were passed in making short excursions to the neighboring plantations, went swiftly enough, but their nights seemed somewhat long. On one of these, when the wind blew high and threatened a storm, they were gathered together in the parlor, at an early hour. Clara half reclined upon a pine sofa, covered with a mat made of cocoa-nut leaves, and rested her beautiful head upon one of its cushions. "The time passed in yawning ought not to be reckoned in our existence," she remarked to Fernando, who sat at the other end of the sofa reading, by the light of a candle, certain letters which he had just received from Seville; "for to grow old and feel *ennui* at the same time is rather too much of a good thing!"

"Do not yawn, then, Clara," said her cousin, smiling.

"Goodness me!" exclaimed Clara, "in this rattletrap of a house, where every thing seems sleepy and sombre, who can help it, I should like to know? One would suppose that instead of being a favorite of the court, you had passed all your life in Seville, which seems to delight, like an Indian Brahmin, in its immobility, and rejoice, as an owl, in its obscurity!"

"At the risk, then, of appearing an obscure Sevillano, I must say, cousin, that I often felt *bored* at the court, and never feel so here."

"*Chacun à son gout*," answered Clara.

"So long as I am by your side, Clara, I cannot feel otherwise than happy."

"I regret Fernando," Clara rejoined, "that, although I love you dearly, I cannot return the compliment.—Carlos," she added, turning toward her other cousin, who was stirring the fire, "what a smoke you are raising! Of the three characters who are said not to excel in making a fire—a poet, a lover, and a madman—I think you have the best claim to the last."

"I rather prefer to be reckoned among the first and second," replied Carlos; "but it is not my fault that the chimney smokes; that properly belongs to its maker."

Maria, who never let slip an opportunity of seeing what was going on in the family, now entered, crying out "My stars! how bad the Englishman smells!" She had given this name to a mechanical lamp that the countess had bought in London for her aunt, which, placed on the mantel-piece, threw its full light on an English periodical which Doctor Narciso, with his back to the chimney, was attentively reading. These lamps had just then been introduced into Spain, to the great annoyance of all the indigenous Pedros and Marias, who could not understand their complicated mechanism; and this night Maria was quite right in her remark, for the badly trimmed "Englishman" emitted a most insupportable odor.

"Oh, countess!" exclaimed Narciso, suddenly, and with such vehemence that he made the Asistenta and Elia leap from their seats.

"What has happened?" asked the former.

"The most marvellous discovery has been made in this island, not of swans, as the poet says, but of Titans, as the plain truth proves. Steam-power has been used successfully in manufacturing cloth."

"What men, what geniuses!" said the countess, abstractedly, without feeling the slightest interest in the discovery.

"And what does it amount to, that you are in this ecstasy over it?" asked the Asistenta.

"Señora," replied the enthusiastic philosopher, "think of the economy of labor which dispenses with two hundred strong arms in a single factory! He who conceived and carried out such a magnificent idea deserves—"

"To be hung!" cried the Asistenta, finishing the sentence for him.

Doctor Narciso had just opened his mouth, in readiness to make an eloquent harangue in favor of moral and material advancement, when a fresh cloud of smoke set him to coughing and sneezing together.

"In no other country but Spain," said he at length, " where people live *à la lazzaroni*, could such detestable country-houses be found. There is here an inertia, a *sans-souci*, which throws the Turks and Indians into the background. It is not merely a *stand-still*, it is a retrograde, a marching backward. I trust I shall one day see Cadiz, which the Andalusians, with their usual boastfulness, call a silver cup. I warrant I'll find it more like a potter's mug."

" Oh, do hush, Narciso!" said the countess, who was justly provoked at the rudeness of her Hippocrates. "I have heard you grumble enough. In London you were in despair; in Paris raging, just as you are here; and no doubt will be when you get to Cadiz!"

"Don't you remember," said Carlos, " the story of the man who was continually changing his residence because he had a spectre in his house, and who one day had all his effects on a cart to move as usual, when lo and behold, he espied, on his dining-table, the spectre, with a horrible grin on his skeleton face, dancing a rigadoon with a queer little fellow resembling a *monkey on hoofs?*"

"So that he carried his evil spirit always with him," said Clara, laughing, "with the old gentleman in black to boot."

"Exactly so, cousin."

"You should remember, countess" said Narciso, "that I was suffering from rheumatism in England; and in Paris, that cradle of liberalism and philosophy, sacred lights of society!—I was shocked to see so much bigotry and superstition."

"And how were they manifested?" asked the Asistenta.

"Señora, those worldly people, seekers of pleasure and followers of fashion, joined in religious processions, and actually thronged the churches."

"And they did well," said the Asistenta; "for the temple of God is the refuge of the sinner, as well as the home of the saint."

"But, señora, many were hypocrites."

"Let them go to church nevertheless," rejoined the Asistenta.

"Many went to hear the music."

"Let them enter."

"Some solely to see the stained-glass windows."

"Let them enter."

" Others to burlesque and criticise."

" Like yourself, Doctor Narciso; these last are the only ones to whom the church should be closed."

" And to all others open?"

"Yes, a thousand times yes—for look you here, doctor; each one who enters God's house uncovers His head, and there comes a solemn moment when all bend the knee before His Divine Majesty who then sees thousands prostrate at His feet—and respect, even if it be shown only in outward forms, has its merit. And why should not the lukewarm and indifferent mingle with the devout? Is not virtue as well as vice contagious? Who knows but there may be distilled from the hearts of the vain and frivolous, upon bending the knee, and under the impression of the general reverence, a drop of divine adoration! Certain sinful men, it seems to me, are more exacting than the good God, and the spotless Saviour of mankind."

"You are a *Molinista* of the worst type," sneered the doctor.

" What do you mean by that, sir?" exclaimed the Asistenta, sharply. "I am nothing, I'd have you to know, that cannot be expressed in intelligible language."

"I mean you have too much charity for others by far, señora."

"Because I need it for myself, Doctor Narciso. We must not expect too much from others. Let us teach by example, rather than precept. Instead of placing intolerance and austerity like two sentinels at the door of the church, I would place over it this inscription: 'The house of our common Father, always open, and open to all.'"

"Open to all," repeated Elia, with the sympathy of an angel of heaven for the erring and afflicted.

"Open to all," said Don Benigno, with the indulgence of a good man for the weakness of his fellows.

"Open to all," exclaimed Maria, with the fervent zeal of a Catholic, "to unite all the earth at the foot of one altar, in one faith, one hope, one baptism."

"If you believe," said the doctor, "that, by smiting yourself on the breast and praying, you can enter the kingdom of heaven only—"

"By this alone?—no," interrupted the Asistenta; "but without this, no one is saved; for salvation is not a right, but a favor. No one, by acts alone, can merit it, but must on bended knees implore it."

"Señora," replied Narciso, with affected dignity, "God makes man suffer in this world and owes him a compensation in the next. To think otherwise is absurd."

"Owes him!" exclaimed the Asistenta, "owes him! So you have only to treat God as you treat kings nowadays. Restrict his rights, limit his powers, and prescribe his duties; and make him, if it were possible, conform to a written constitution and recognize the rights of man—rebellion, all of it—pure spirit of rebellion!"

"The very name of king," rejoined Narciso, who seemed anxious to shift his ground, "insults the dignity of man. The great Voltaire has said that 'the first king was a victorious soldier.'"

"Voltaire lied!" cried the Asistenta, warmly. "This can be said of the first tyrant. The first king was a patriarch."

"Who says so?"

"I say so!"

"Permit me to say to you, señora, that to dispute the authority of such men as Voltaire, Diderot, Helvetius, Rousseau, D'Alembert—"

"The devil and his followers!" exclaimed the Asistenta, "who with their infamous doctrines are the Neros and Diocletians of this century. But, my friend, as much as it may displease you and these other disciples, we will ultimately triumph over them. Isn't it so, my children?"

"We will triumph, we will triumph!" shouted all in fervent chorus.

At this moment Pedro entered to announce supper.

"Isn't it wonderful, Pedro," said Maria to him, after the family had left the parlor, "to see how our mistress, who scarcely ever looks at a book, puts to shame that renegade Spaniard, who does nothing but read?"

While they were passing through the hall, Carlos said to Elia, "I also wish to triumph, Elia."

"Over your evil passions, Carlos?"

"No, I have no evil passions, Elia—I wish to triumph over your convent, which is a Minotaur."

"And what is that, pray?"

"The Minotaur was a monster, who devoured maidens by hundreds."

"You are thinking of your regiment, which devoured so many of our young men, Carlos. As to the convent, you know about as much of it as a crow does of music." So saying, Elia tapped him lightly on the head with her fan, and, with a merry laugh ran to the Asistenta.

CHAPTER IX.

For two days the rain poured in torrents, but on the third the sun broke through the clouds, and the country looked as fresh and smiling as an Eastern beauty emerging from a perfumed bath.

It was determined to dine, on the morrow, at a plantation belonging to the Asistenta, distant about a league from the village; and the good woman was in her room, making preparations for the excursion.

"Shall I have an ox killed, señora?" asked Pedro.

"No," cried the officious Maria, "a lamb!"

"An ox would be better," returned Pedro, "for there will be a hundred persons in all."

But Maria persisted in insisting upon having a lamb for the *olla,* so that quite a violent altercation ensued between herself and the worthy steward.

"Stop quarrelling," said the Asistenta, "and let us have both beef and mutton, Pedro!"

"Through the obstinacy of this woman," growled Pedro, "the señora is led into useless extravagance."

"And she will not miss a lamb from her large flock, nor a dozen lambs, for the matter of that," retorted Maria.

"A robber's proverb, truly," objected Pedro. "How very liberal you are, Madame Bountiful, with others' property!"

"You two are always quarrelling," intervened the Asistenta; "you either love or hate each other greatly—I don't know which."

"You may believe in our eternal dislike, señora," said Maria, "for our angels are surely at variance."

"Your ladyship," added Pedro, "I am the beef, and Maria the butcher's knife."

"You are quite right," returned Maria, "in calling yourself *beef*, for, through idleness and good living, you have become as round as a fatted ox."

"And you," rejoined Pedro, "with the fiery temper which consumes you, are like a stringed bean, and about as yellow as a parched pea."

"Why don't you marry?" asked their mistress. "There would be peace between you then, by night at least."

"With this woman, señora, there can be no peace. I warrant, instead of snoring at night, she grumbles."

"I have been married once," said Maria, "but if I had not been, I would die an old maid before marrying this fellow."

"I too have been married," cried Pedro, "and I would not marry a second time if the Princess of the Asturias were offered to me as a bride, remembering, as I do, that story—"

"For Heaven's sake, Pedro," interrupted Maria, "let us have none of your stories!"

"Let me hear it, Pedro," said the Asistenta.

"Well, my lady, there were two friends, Juan Castaños and Guillermo Pons, who vowed a vow that the first who died should return and inform the other how it fared with him in the next world. Both were married, and, in process of time, it happened that Pons died, and, a few nights after his death, appeared to his friend. 'How goes it with you?' asked Castaños. 'Grandly!' answered the apparition. 'When I presented myself on high, Saint Peter asked me, "What sort of a life have you led upon the earth?" "Señor," I replied, "I am a poor man. I was married to—" "Say not another word," interrupted his saintship, "having passed through purgatory, you are entitled to paradise." So I am now in glory; good-night.'

"Time passed; Juan lost his wife, and married a second time, and, finally, his own hour came. After he had been carried out of his house, feet foremost, he presented himself with a very bold face at the gates of heaven.

"'What has been your life on earth?' asked the saintly gate-keeper. 'I have been twice married,' answered Juan briskly, taking a step forward to go in. But the bald-headed saint, giving him a rap on his head with his key, cried out: 'Stand back, friend; heaven was not made for *fools*.'"

"Do you wish a receipt for that story, Pedro?" asked Maria. "I can certify to having heard you repeat it at least twenty times. It is as old as the hills."

"Would you like to hear a new one?"

"God forbid, if you are to tell it?"

Pedro was just opening his mouth to commence anew, when the Asistenta cut him short with—

"Maria, remember that spices do not agree with Clara."

"I will bear it in mind, señora."

"Pedro, my nephews are very fond of ginger-cakes."

"I know it, your ladyship."

"Be sure, Maria, that you have orange-jelly for Elia, lemonade for Don Benigno, and a number of bottles of claret for Doctor Delgado."

"Gracious me, señora, if that grumbling doctor cannot drink our sherry, let him have vinegar!"

"Doctor Delgado is our guest, Maria," said the Asistenta, reprovingly, and rising to leave the room, "and should be treated as such."

"She thinks of every one but herself," said Maria, after her mistress had departed; "if you had not provided a turkey, Pedro, and I the calves-foot jelly, she would not have any thing to eat to-morrow."

On the following morning, bright and early, a large number of little angels, not reckoned among the *good*, gathered in the court-yard, to get another look at the bob-tails, to which they had given the name of frogs; but in this they were disappointed, as the whole party went on mule-back, with the exception of Fernando and Carlos, who rode the colts, and Pedro, who mounted a sorry old horse, afflicted with the spavin and heaves. The countess was seated in a superb saddle of red morocco; but the Asistenta and Elia were content with the common wooden saddle of the country, made in the form of a cross.

"Oh, Tough-hide!" cried one of the muleteers, placing a basket of provisions on his flinching mule, "it seems that you are not willing to carry this basket, which is as light as a nun's heart, although you are able to bear the weight of the Giralda."* Saying this, he gave the poor animal a blow which fairly took the skin off its loins.

* The tower in the cathedral.

"For God's sake," cried Elia, moved to tears by the suffering of the animal, "do not beat your mule so!"

"He does not understand any other language," replied the man.

"It is barbarous," said the Asistenta, "to treat an animal that helps you to gain your daily bread, with such cruelty."

"If he had been born a bishop," said the man, sullenly, "I would cover him with benedictions."

"Well, you must not whip him so here," rejoined the Asistenta, warmly; "either give up your whip, or leave the court-yard."

The muleteer, without replying, began to unload his mule.

"Señora," said the overseer, in a low voice to the Asistenta, "because an ass gives a kick, would you cut his leg off? This poor man has a wife and six children to support."

"Well, let him go with us, then, but he must give up his whip."

"You hear what our lady says, Miguel—come, load your beast again."

"If the basket waits till I take it," answered

Miguel, "it will be here at the day of judgment."

"Don't be foolish, Miguel," whispered the overseer, "ten shillings are not to be found every day; and then we will have wine and meat in abundance."

"I would not go if the king ordered me," was the reply. "No one need tell me twice to go away. I eat my bread with honor, or suffer hunger patiently." So saying, the muleteer gave his mule a furious blow, and rode away.

"Did you ever see such a proud vagabond?" said the Asistenta. "I should like to give him a dozen blows with that whip which he uses so liberally on his beast. But his wife and children must not suffer. Send them a dollar, Frasco, and be sure not to let them know where it comes from."

"A genuine Andalusian!" sneered Delgado, "poor as Job, proud as Tarquin."

"Honor and profit are not found in one sack," said the overseer, speaking up for the honor of his countrymen.

"You are right, Frasco," cried the countess, enthusiastically. "These men have the souls of princes under the garb of peasants. Send him a half ounce for me."

"That is not right, señora countess," remarked the overseer, with great good sense; "the sum is too large."

But the countess, without heeding him, rode off at full speed.

The day was beautiful. Higher than ever appeared the celestial vault, clearer the atmosphere, more brilliant the sun. The birds were flitting to and fro, and singing merrily in the smiling fields which were hedged in with aloes, standing stately and stiff like sentries on post, and protecting with their shade wild roses of every shade of color; and even the rough and sterile bridle-path which our pleasure-seekers were pursuing gave birth to the sweet-smelling, white-flowered thyme, which filled the air with its delicious fragrance.

The scenes of nature make a profound impression upon those persons who, by reading and culture, have enlarged the limits of their sensations, and upon those who have experienced either great joy or great sorrow. But those whose past and present are uniform and tranquil, and who have not lost in naturalness and grace what they have gained in elegance and polish, admire and enjoy nature, without having their hearts greatly moved by it. And as our party (Narciso excepted) belonged to this latter class, they went along treading upon flowers and breathing their perfume, with the enjoyment of a troop of children issuing from a schoolroom on the eve of a long vacation.

"Have you many children, José?" asked the Asistenta, addressing the man who had charge of the mule which she was riding.

"Eight, señora."

"Do you love them much?"

"Señora, as many as are born are loved."

"Boys or girls?"

"Five boys and three girls, señora: the two eldest boys have been conscripted, the third is in your service, and the youngest are swineherds."

"They are no longer an expense to you, then?"

"True, señora; but you know the saying,

> 'A hungry wife and daughters three,
> No sadder sight for man to see.'"

"If I remember aright, I advanced you money last year?"

"Yes, your ladyship; and if I have not returned it—"

"Never mind that, never mind that," interrupted the Asistenta, hurriedly.

"Well, señora, the past season nothing went well with me. My donkey took the distemper and died—a drought destroyed my hay and corn—and a neighbor's pigs devoured all my vegetables."

"Goodness me! man, every thing seems indeed to have gone wrong with you."

"There is a saint, señora, in heaven, called San Guilindron, who ever, while he dances before the throne, sings—

'The petition of the poor,
Let it not reach heaven's door.'"

"Fortune is not always found by those who seek it, that is certain, my good José."

"You have not heard all yet, my lady. In the fall we all fell ill with the ague. His Divine Majesty is ever saying, 'Give him more.' 'Señor,' says Saint Good Fortune to Him, 'the Duke of Medina Sidonia has drawn a prize in the lottery.' 'Give him more,' says His Majesty. 'Poor Juan Quevedo,' cries the saint again, 'has been beaten with stripes.' 'Give him more,' is the commandment."

"José, our Father in heaven does all things wisely and well."

"In the other world we will know it, señora."

"This year you shall have another advance, and the first I consider cancelled. Frasco will give you, too, a donkey and a couple of pigs."

"Now may God bless your ladyship! well have you been called the friend of the poor."

Don Benigno followed close to his lady, and, with his accustomed parsimony of words, only said from time to time—

"José, take care of that stump; José, this hill is slippery; José, there is a ditch on the right; José, don't the girths need tightening?"

Elia preceded them, happier than the sun, her lap filled with flowers, which her muleteer had cut for her.

"Look at these beautiful flowers," said she to Carlos, who never left her side. "This is *yerba buena*: this *mejor ana*. Do you know why it is so called?"

"No, do you?"

"Yes; one day San Joaquin and Santa Ana were gathering herbs. Santa Ana found the former, and said to her husband, 'Joaquin, this is *yerba buena*;'* but the saint, who had found the other, handed it to her, and replied, 'This is *mejor Ana.*†'"

"They are very pretty, Elia, but I admire most the beautiful red rose which you wear in your hair, under your white veil, and which is so becoming to you that I am at a loss to know whether it is you who embellish these fields or the fields that beautify you."

"It is the rose of Jericho," said Elia. "There was a rose-bush at the foot of the cross whose roses were white; a drop of the precious blood of our Lord fell upon a rose, and gave it this divine color."

"What a *salmagundi* of superstitious nonsense!" exclaimed Delgado, whose mule, being from the same stable as Elia's, had been gradually approaching it. "Of what avail is it to establish free schools among a people who have their chronicles and etymologics, and even their faith,

* A good herb.   † Better Anna.

handed down to them in flowers, plants, rhymes, and stories? How could the plants *yerba buena* and *mejor ana* have got their names as you suppose, when San Joaquin and Santa Ana did not speak Spanish?"

"Did not speak Spanish!" cried Elia; "what did they speak, French?"

"No, señorita, they spoke Hebrew. Don't forget this, which will be more useful for you to believe than the stuff I heard you telling Carlos, yesterday, about the passion-flower, that it contained all the instruments used at the passion of our Saviour. It is a shocking irreverence to talk thus."

"Perhaps God has made the flower thus," said Elia, "to remind us of our Saviour's sufferings, or may be it grows so of itself to honor Him."

"Cease your prattle," cried the doctor, impatiently. "Can you suppose that flowers have a will of their own, or that God gives understanding to plants which jackasses eat? Reflect and reason a little."

At this instant the doctor's mule stumbled, and threw him over his head into the road.

"Curses on you!" said he, rising and brushing the dirt from his face, amid the general laughter, "this mode of diverting one's self, in this outlandish hole, is more than vulgar—it is villanous!"

"You may consider your fall a punishment from the gods," said Carlos, "for throwing cannon-balls against the butterflies resting so gracefully upon Elia's vermilion lips, as upon a rose."

Don Narciso replied not; but, in a very bad humor, remounted his mule, and, curbing him violently, compelled him to drop astern, as a sailor would say, until he brought up with the rear-guard, composed of Pedro and Maria.

"Señor," said his attendant to him, after a long silence, "have you ever seen the estates about here? Romeral is the most famous. Three hundred acres of land in a park, a plantation of young olives, and farm-houses that look like a monastery. In all this section—"

"Hold your tongue!" cried the doctor, interrupting him. "Every reasoning being requires some hours a day for reflection. You have just cut the thread of my thoughts with your confounded clack! What do you suppose I care about estates that are not mine?"

The poor muleteer cast an envious glance upon José, to whom the Asistenta, that great and powerful lady, was so kindly and encouragingly talking. "How great is the difference between Mistress Somebody and Mister Nobody!" said he to himself.

"You have forgotten the toothpicks, Pedro," said Maria, at this instant. "Your memory is like a sieve."

"They are not needed," said Narciso, shouting in her ear. "In England it is considered bad manners to use them at dinner, and besides, they ruin the gums."

"I thought," muttered Maria, "that we could not get through the day without having England thrown in our teeth!"

"Pedro, have you brought any claret?" asked Narciso.

"Yes, señor, a half dozen bottles."

"Pedro has a good memory for liquor," growled Maria, sarcastically.

"Certainly," returned the ungallant Pedro, "for Father Thomas says that St. Paul took a little wine for his stomach's sake, and it is an old saying, 'Water for horses, wine for men, and a rod for women and donkeys.'"

"And a famous English poet also writes," chimed in the learned and amiable Narciso—

"'A woman, a dog, and a walnut-tree,
　The more you thrash them, the better they be.'"

"Clara," said Carlos, pointing to Pedro and the doctor, "Don Quixote and Sancho Panza have changed animals, I perceive."

CHAPTER X.

THEY had now entered an olive-grove, and the white walls surrounding the plantation of Romeral, so extolled by the doctor's muleteer, began to appear through the dense foliage of the trees. In front of the grand old farm-house stood an enormous mulberry-tree, a giant of the forest, raised by the hand of Time. Against its trunk rested a rude plough; from its branches hung a musket and a guitar, and under its shade a man of robust frame and animated countenance carelessly reclined, who, it was easily to be seen, could and would use any one of the three, as circumstances might require. He rose quickly as the Asistenta approached, and called loudly, "Beatriz!" when a woman came out of the farm-house with a chair in her hand, which she hastened to place so that her mistress might alight from her mule easily.

"Thanks be to God, my lady," said she, fervently, "who has permitted me to see you to-day! How fares it with your ladyship?"

"As with all the girls of my time, Beatriz, who have lived many years, and have but few left upon the earth. And you, woman, how goes it with you? And your mother, and your children? Has the one who broke his arm recovered?"

She said this ascending the staircase, in the interior of the house, and entering into a long parlor, provided with a few broken chairs, a pine table, and a bare floor.

"My God! aunt," exclaimed the countess, "this seems like a plundered hospital."

"And why should I furnish houses in which I pass a couple of hours about every three years?" asked the Asistenta.

They seated themselves, and partook of orangeade and lemonade, and, missing Delgado, looked out of a window, and beheld him, like a second Pickwick, kneeling upon the ground, with his nose in close proximity to an old stone, which he was examining with the closest attention. In a moment or two he jumped to his feet, with an exultant smile on his face, and ran into the house as fast as his frail under-pinning would allow him.

"Señora," he exclaimed with emphasis, "I have just found a treasure, the stone over a Roman grave, with its inscription. Did you know that you possessed such a jewel?"

"No," answered the Asistenta, "and I am sure I don't care what was placed over the sepulchre of a pagan."

"Who discovered it?" asked the enthusiastic doctor.

"How should I know?" replied the Asistenta, coolly.

"They found it," said Beatriz, "while digging a hole to burn lime in, and my husband brought it here that it might serve as a threshold for the stable door."

"O stupid ignorance!" exclaimed Delgado, full of antiquarian fire. "Didn't your husband see the Latin inscription, woman?"

"My husband does not know how to read," said the farmer's wife, meekly. "He was left an orphan when quite a little child, and has had to work hard all his life."

Fernando and Carlos, who had gone out to look at the stone, now returned.

"It is certainly Roman," said the former. "The inscription has been rudely dealt with by its finders, but the letters S. T. T. L. are plainly to be seen."

"Do you hear, señora? The appreciable S. T. T. L.," cried Don Narciso, looking triumphantly at the Asistenta.

"And what do the appreciable S. T. T. L. signify?"

"*Sit tibi terra levis:* 'May the earth be light upon thee!'"

"Why, that's nonsense!"

"Señora, señora, Roman literature, the sanction of ages, the admiration of *savants*, is all included in your sweeping assertion."

"And yet I must repeat it without being imposed upon by your didactic tone or highflown expressions. And to prove that I am correct, I have but to compare your appreciable letters S. T. T. L. with those the Catholic faith places over sepulchres, namely: R. I. P. A. *Requiescat in pace, Amen!* 'May he rest in peace, Amen!'—a solemn prayer to God for the immortal soul; while the pagan's is an invocation to the *earth* that it may be as light as a rope-dancer, and not bear heavily on bones and dust! What think you of it, Don Benigno?"

"That it would not apply to one buried in a vault."

"Very true. And you, Maria, who stand there with your eyes and mouth wide open?"

"I think, señora, if there must be something light about it, it would be better to say: 'May your sins be light upon you!'"

"And you say well, woman, much better than the *savants*, for in matters relating to the soul, and the other world, there is no wisdom outside of the Church. And you, my child, what think you of the appreciable S. T. T. L. which so fills Doctor Narciso with admiration?"

"They do not awake in me the thoughts which seem appropriate to death."

"Well, what would you place over a tomb, my little lady?" asked Narciso, in a mocking voice—"you who pretend to excel the Romans?"

"I would place over it," said Elia, softly, "a

little verse which the lady abbess was in the habit of repeating when we spoke of death:

> 'Be lowly, that you may be exalted:
> Lose, that you may gain;
> Die, yet live.'"

"Very well, my darling," cried the Asistenta. "I see that we all know more than those learned Romans, simply by being instructed in the Catholic faith. Your husband did right, Beatriz. Let the stone remain as a threshold for the stable."

"But, señora," said the doctor, "if you do not value it, you should sell it, for it will bring a great price."

"I do not care to sell it."

"Give it to me then, aunt," cried Clara.

"I am not in the humor of giving," replied the Asistenta, who was evidently bent upon destroying the appreciable S. T. T. L.

"How obstinate aunt is!" whispered Clara to Carlos, who was standing by her side.

"As a proprietor of landed property, she naturally does not like *light earth*," replied Carlos.

"No, nor heavy nephews," said the Asistenta, who had overheard him.

"What a pity, Clara," continued Carlos, "that our friend Sir Arthur Sidney, who was so enthusiastic about antiquities, is not here!"

"Is he the violinist who was at Clara's dinner-party?" asked the Asistenta.

"No, indeed, aunt; a young Englishman of distinction, the son of a bishop."

"The son of a bishop! what are you dreaming about, child?"

"In England, my dear aunt, bishops are permitted to marry."

"What an impudent falsehood! Do you suppose you can make me believe that there is a country under the sun where bishops marry? Come, sir, this is a little too much!"

"Upon my word, aunt, you call one a cheat with all the ease in the world. I tell you again that in England the bishops marry, and not only they, but the canons, chaplains, and curates. If you don't believe me, ask Clara."

"It is so, aunt, I assure you," said Clara. "The English are not *papists*, remember, as they call us, and can—"

"And you too, Clara?" interrupted the Asistenta. "Are you mad, or do you wish to make me so? A *bishopress!* a *bishopress!* Don Benigno, can you conceive of a bishopress?"

"No, señora, nor of a curatess."

"When we return to Seville, señora," said the doctor, compassionately, "I will show you the 'English Peerage,' in which are noted officially all the noble families, with their connections and intermarriages, and among them you will see, in black and white, that of the bishops."

"May you live a thousand years!" replied the Asistenta, laconically.

"There are none so blind as those who will not see, aunt," said Carlos, "and therefore—"

But the countess, interrupting him, whispered in his ear—

"Don't insist, cousin. You cannot convince her; and what harm can result from her believing that bishops cannot marry?"

"Well, for my part," said Fernando, "I must confess to a feeling of the highest veneration, at beholding such a proof of the exalted and almost ideal dignity which our bishops have been able to give to the mitre, as it is exhibited by aunt's refusal to believe what Carlos tells her. This instinctive faith of hers, which elevates these worthy prelates above all passion, all love, all the personal relations of earth, proves more, in favor of the institution and the individuals, than the most eloquent arguments of our finest orators."

"But, marquis," said Narciso, "you must confess that it is sheer obstinacy to cling thus to error, especially when she is told that we are not speaking of Catholics."

"This holy respect of aunt's, doctor, extends even to the *name* of bishop, which she cannot separate from Catholicism. And this is grand under the aspect of faith, and beautiful under that of fidelity, and claims my sympathy. To tell the honest truth, I envy aunt, who listens to a fact which does not surprise us, as a profanation, a fanciful creation. How true it is that the more one knows, the less one feels!"

"It is better to know than to feel," said the enlightened doctor.

"Not so," cried Carlos, "I would give all my books for a sentiment."

"Above all, in matters of religion," said Fernando; "the faith of the heart is voluntary, that of the brain compulsory."

After they had partaken of refreshments, the whole party sallied forth for a walk. Fernando offered his arm to his aunt.

"No, my son," said she; "leave me with Don Benigno, who is accustomed to my gait. I shall not walk far, so go with the others. I charge you, however, to look out for Elia. She runs too much, and this hot sun may give her a fever."

Don Benigno opened an immense red umbrella, capable of protecting a dozen persons, and held it over his mistress, while the overseer walked a little in advance. "Señora," said the former, "Frasco and I have been thinking that there are too many hands employed here, whose wages might be saved. The services of several of the muleteers and shepherds, for instance, might be dispensed with."

"That is very true," replied the Asistenta; "there is one thing, however, that you have forgotten."

"And what is that, señora?" asked both in a breath.

"The important fact that, although I can do without these men, they cannot get along without me. So let every thing remain as it is."

While this conversation was going on, Elia was running like a deer, examining trees, culling flowers, and keeping ahead of everybody, except Carlos, who never lost sight of her for an instant.

"Look," said she, handing him a bell-shaped flower, "at this old woman's candle."

"I would rather behold the light from your beautiful eyes," said Carlos, passionately.

"Look here, Carlos," she answered, "you have of late done nothing but flatter me. How would you like to be praised continually to your face?"

"Very much, if you were the praiser."

"Well, you are a presumptuous fellow. So you like flattery, do you?"

"Out of your mouth, yes."

"And why out of my mouth?"

"Because I love you, Elia, with my whole heart; not as a sister or a friend, but as the body loves the soul, without which it cannot exist. Will you love me in return, Elia?"

A confusion, strange for her, took possession of Elia, upon hearing these sweet but passionate words, as she took a half step backward and cast her eyes to the ground.

"Do you believe me, my Elia?" asked Carlos, in a voice profoundly moved.

Elia, reproaching herself for having involuntarily shrunk, like the sensitive plant, at the first love-throb of her heart, now fixed her large black eyes on Carlos, and, with the candor and sweetness of an angel, replied:

"Yes, I believe you; Carlos, why should I not believe you?"

"And you, Elia," continued Carlos, in a soft and trembling tone, "can you, will you love me as I love you?"

Elia's face and neck were suffused with crimson, and her lips quivered, as she artlessly replied:

"I love you so dearly, Carlos, that I could not live in the world without you, but should be obliged to fly for refuge to the convent."

"I swear to you, then," said Carlos, solemnly, and placing a gold ring on her finger as he spoke, "and I call upon God your Father and the angels your brothers as witnesses, to love you always, to unite my lot with yours, to be your companion and protector, and to share with you loyally the pains and joys of life."

"That is, you will be my husband, Carlos?"

"On the honor of a soldier and a nobleman."

"How happy mother will be when I tell her!"

"You must not say a word to her on the subject," exclaimed the young man, hastily.

"And why, Carlos?"

"Because—because—because it is customary for men to speak of such matters to their parents before others are informed of them."

"I feel that you are right, Carlos, but you must speak to your mother at once; for I cannot long keep any thing from mine."

"I must prepare her mind for the announcement, Elia. I cannot break it to her suddenly."

"Prepare her mind, Carlos—what do you mean?"

"Because, my little innocent, mothers do not generally like their sons to marry, especially at my age."

"What! mothers do not like their sons to

marry?—you surprise me. A secret, a secret!" she continued, sadly.

"Elia, do you not think a love-secret, like ours, sweet!"

"The love, yes, Carlos—the secret, no!"

"Why, my darling?"

"Because every thing is most beautiful, Carlos, in the clear light of day; because a secret in the heart is like a stain on a crystal, which mars its beauty and deprives it of its transparency."

At this moment, Fernando, who was looking for Elia, as his aunt had requested, came out suddenly from behind the olive-trees.

Elia, instinctively abashed, turned and fled; Carlos, surprised, remained silent.

"Carlos! Carlos!" said his brother, in a tone of bitter reproof, "this is not the conduct of a gentleman."

"What do you mean?" asked Carlos, angrily.

"I mean that it is cruel, Carlos, to turn the head of a young girl, an angel of innocence, with hopes that can never be realized, and not remember that, while the roses are yours, the thorns will all be hers."

"You do me injustice, Fernando: in proof of it, I will tell you that I have just sworn to make Elia my wife."

Fernando, upon hearing this, seemed like one in a dream. The invincible obstacles which presented themselves to his brother's designs, the discord and unhappiness which he foresaw in consequence, terrified him; on the other hand, the satisfaction he felt on finding his brother, although as thoughtless and impulsive as ever, as ever noble and honorable, disarmed him, and so, laying his hand on his shoulder, he said: "Pardon me, brother, if I have been unjust; but you should at least have remembered, before addressing Elia, that what you propose is impossible, and, if you persist in it, will only work her unhappiness and your own."

"And why?"

"Because Elia, the foundling, ought not, cannot, and will not be the wife of an Orrea!"

"Elia," Carlos answered, "is too little versed in the customs of the world, even to suspect that the want of a patent of nobility can raise a barrier between two persons who love each other; and as for me, I despise such *effete* notions."

"*Effete* notions!" echoed Fernando. "Know, my brother, that there are trees with roots so firmly planted in the ground, that although they may be cut down, they will spring up again with renewed life, because the sap is in the bowels of Mother Earth—Carlos, you cannot set society at defiance."

"What care I for its verdict?"

"No one is above the opinion of the world," answered Fernando. "To think otherwise, is to deceive one's-self. Follow the advice of a brother who loves you with his whole heart. Fly, Carlos, and sacrifice passion to reason."

"What religion, what code of morality, what duty imposes upon me this sacrifice? upon what altar shall I offer up Elia's happiness and my own?" asked Carlos passionately.

"We are far from understanding each other," replied Fernando with dignity, "if all the duties of an illustrious house, of a gentleman, and of a man of refinement and sensibility are confined in your opinion to the religious and moral. Leaving this ground, where your blind passion separates us, let me remind you, Carlos, that you are digging your mother's grave!"

Carlos stood aghast and silent for a moment; and then, leaning his burning head upon his brother's shoulder, he sobbed rather than said: "No, no, Fernando, mother is too good and just to sacrifice this pure angel to her vanity and pride. And you, who have been my protector and guide, will you not befriend me now?"

"With all the power I can command, Carlos. But I prefer to snatch you alive from a precipice rather than to drag you wounded and bleeding from an abyss."

CHAPTER XI.

While the scene we have described in the preceding chapter was passing between the brothers, one of a very different character was taking place between the Asistenta and a multitude of ragged, dirty beings, who, surrounding her, and gesticulating violently, cried out in discordant tones, "Prisoner! prisoner!"

The singular part of the whole affair was, that the Asistenta's face, far from expressing terror or indignation, seemed beaming with pleasure.

"Let them alone, Frasco," said she to the overseer, who was endeavoring to disperse the crowd; "they are only claiming their dues."

'Booty! booty!" cried the ragamuffins.

"Will you be still?" cried Frasco.

"Did I not tell you to let them alone, you obstinate fellow you?" said the Asistenta.

"They will not have to take me to jail, for I here offer a lamb for my ransom."

"Good! good!" shouted the crowd, "but the secretary is our prisoner!"

Don Benigno was about taking a dollar from his purse, when the Asistenta stopped him, by pledging a calf as his ransom.

At this there was a terrific explosion of happiness. There were no *vivas*, but an infinity of—"*May God repay you!*"

"Señora, señora," said the economical secretary, in a piteous tone, "I am not worth a calf."

"But I am certainly worth more than a lamb," replied his mistress, "so one will be an offset for the other.—Good-day, my children; Frasco will see that you are paid."

This legion of *robber-beggars* consisted of those engaged in gathering olives, who are, for the most part, old men and women, and children of both sexes, between the detestable ages of ten and fourteen, and all miserably poor. They are clothed in rags and sleep in the fields, or in the streets of the village to which they belong. They had made a prisoner of the Asistenta; this being their recognized manner, according to the custom prevailing among them, from time immemorial, of exacting alms.

When the party returned to the farm-house, dinner was served.

"Delgado," said the countess, "I really have an appetite, and I do believe I can eat *olla!*"

"You have been getting better," said Maria, "ever since Doña Isabel prayed for you to San Antonio."

"What stuff and nonsense!" growled the doctor.

"Señor," said the Asistenta, impatiently, "I begin to think you are an infidel. Let me see, now: do you believe in God?"

"But, señora," said the philosopher, "it appears to me that this examination is out of place here, to say the least of it."

"Answer! answer!" retorted the Asistenta, "for I am very curious, as all old women are, and I insist upon knowing."

"Yes, then, señora, yes; I believe in a Supreme Being."

"Rather indefinite; but proceed. Do you believe there is a heaven?"

"I believe in the mansion of the just."

"Do you believe in prayer and its efficacy?"

"I believe we should sing praises to the Divine Maker, as the birds do at the dawn of day."

"Beautiful models of devotion, truly! But the efficacy of prayer?"

"I do not believe in its immediate effect. It is great arrogance to believe that the *Divinity* is so far taken up with us that He intervenes even in our private affairs."

"Why do you pray, then?"

"My prayer is a hymn of thanksgiving and praise."

"With Alexanders, as on my birthday."

"Alexandrines you mean, señora."

"It is all the same to me," answered the Asistenta, "provided I am not obliged to listen to more of them."

The doctor answered gruffly, "I am not a religious poet, madame;" while the Asistenta continued with—

"Your catechism is certainly an original one, but I'll be willing to lose my ears if you can make the people understand it, and my nose to boot if I can comprehend it myself, except that it squares well with your appreciable S. T. T. L. and with the word *agur*, invented by the devil, to avoid saying *á Dios.*"

All burst out laughing at this, except Elia and Carlos, who were too much engrossed with each other to heed what was passing about them. Elia sat silent, wrapped in profound meditation, the present and the future seeming to her all light and happiness; and from time to time a sweet smile stole over her face, such as is seen on the face of a babe when it looks upon its mother or its guardian angel.

Carlos, giving himself up entirely to the present, was wild with happiness. He only saw, he only thought of Elia.

"What a happy day!" he whispered in her ear.

"It is indeed a happy day!" replied Elia, aloud, who had not yet learned that to conceal one's thoughts in society is often necessary and even decorous.

"Does happiness, then, really exist?" asked the misanthropic philosopher; "where is it? what is it? will you be good enough to tell me, my little lady?"

This the amiable gentleman addressed to Elia, who, being considered by him the weakest and most inoffensive of the company, was the one whom he generally attacked with all his forces; but before she could reply, the Asistenta fell upon him, sword in hand, with "Happiness consists in being able and willing to do good to others."

"Gracious, señora!" replied Delgado, "this is virtue, not happiness."

"It consists," said Elia, "in making a pleasure of our duty."

"What do you think of that?" asked the doctor of the countess. "Is it a pleasure, do you suppose, for an artilleryman to place himself in front of the enemy's cannon?"

"Your argument is neither exact nor just, Delgado. There are duties hard and exceptional; but even these afford us pleasure, not in the act of performance, but in the feeling of satisfaction which we enjoy after having performed them. This, however, does not hinder me from agreeing with you, who so well understand the world and the human heart, that real happiness does not exist; and, therefore, we must content ourselves with not expecting it."

"This is high philosophy," said Narciso.

"And you, dear Benigno," said the countess, hurriedly, to avoid an armed intervention which she saw threatening in her aunt's eyes, "in what do you say happiness consists?"

"In not offending God," answered the excellent man, who was not to be prevented by sarcasms from speaking the truth.

"This, doctor," said the Asistenta, "is not what you would consider 'high philosophy,' I suppose; but it certainly is religion of the highest and most exalted character, which is better."

"What a set of stupids, Elia!" whispered Carlos. "Felicity is a love-secret, like ours."

"No, Carlos, no," answered Elia, softly; "a secret is half a lie."

"Happiness," said Fernando, in reply to his aunt, "is the plaything in a child's hands. As soon as he possesses it, he breaks it. So God placed it in hope, which is renewed as often as annihilated."

"Don't deceive yourself, Fernando," replied the Asistenta; "there are people who are never happy, and the fault is with them, not in the world. Happiness is like a good complexion, it comes from the blood."

When Elia about retiring that night she said to Maria:

"Maria, I have two things to tell you: the one must not be told now; the other is, that Doctor Delgado says San Joaquin and Santa Ana did not speak Spanish."

"I am not surprised at that," answered the worthy housekeeper; "for, although born in Spain, he's not a bit better than a foreigner."

CHAPTER XII.

ALL had returned from the country: Carlos with an intense passion, and determined to overcome all obstacles in the way of his happiness; Fernando with great anxiety, and an impatient desire to stop a disastrous current in its devastating course; Clara ready to serve the lovers in their romantic attachment; Doctor Delgado saying "there was nothing so inflammable as the heart of a devotee;" and Maria resolving in her mind that, happen what might, the match should come off. The Asistenta and Don Benigno returned, however, without having noticed any thing; and neither for a moment suspected that the soft and transparent atmosphere in which they lived was charged with the electric fire of tumultuous passions.

The Carnival drew near; it was the Thursday of *Compadres.* The countess, always ready to divert herself, and always taking advantage of her rights as a spoiled child in the house of her aunt, secretly improvised a *soirée* as they say now, or a *sarâo* as it was then called, "to surprise," as she declared, "the dreamy *tertulia* out of its lethargy," as Bonaparte had roused the sleeping Spanish lion from its lair; not with the design, however, of filling *the earth with mortal fear*, but through its brilliancy to fill all Seville with admiration, and make the old *alameda*, with its *immovables*, die with envy. With this object in view, she had invited, for this evening, everybody she could hear of, far and near; so that the Asistenta's parlors were fast filling up with persons she had never seen before. Clara and Carlos, who were observing her look of amazement at each new arrival, were in the "seventh heaven" with delight, and laughing as they had never laughed before.

"This reminds me," said Carlos, "of a good joke some of us young officers played on a storekeeper in Madrid, who kept a store on the corner of Palafox and Medina Streets, with a door opening on each street. Dressed like peasants, we went, one after the other, through the store, entering at one door and going out at the other; each one removing his cap and saluting the storekeeper as he passed by him. When the first one saluted, the storekeeper returned his salute with the utmost courtesy; to the second he remarked that young men were becoming more polite every day; at the third he stared; and at the fourth, who happened to be my unlucky self, he threw a candlestick, while his face wore an expression of astonishment similar to that which aunt's now wears."

While this conversation was going on, the captain-general, who was playing with the Asistenta, remarked, "Señora, you have thrice omitted to follow suit."

"How can I help it, my friend," answered the Asistenta, "when I am all the time bowing to strange people? I am like the king on the throne, receiving persons whom I don't know. I take another card, and go it alone."

"Aunt," said Carlos, approaching her with a fine-looking young officer, who wore the uniform of a lieutenant-colonel, "my friend Riosecco has long desired to know you. His mother was an acquaintance of yours, I think."

"Don't say an acquaintance," answered the Asistenta, "say a very dear friend, whose son I am delighted to see here."

"Aunt," cried Clara in her turn, "permit me to present to you the Count Polikteiski, an unfortunate son of Poland."

"Most happy to see you, sir," said the Asistenta, cordially saluting a very hairy gentleman of florid complexion. "Whose son did she say he was?" after he had passed.

"Of Poland, señora," answered a gentleman near her; "the most rebellious country in the world."

"I thought he had a bad look. I don't see why Clara brought the bear here."

"You lose, señora," said the captain-general.

"Just to think of my losing a game with such cards in my hands!" cried the Asistenta, throwing on the table an ace, two kings, and a knave. "But how can one play in such a Babel as Clara has made my house? God help us! what is this?" she exclaimed, as a band of music struck up in the hall.

At this instant, Elia, accompanied by Carlos

and a crowd of young people, ran to the Asistenta and raising her, almost by force, from her arm-chair carried her into the hall, where a small stage had been erected, on which stood Clara holding by the middle a number of ribbons, whose ends hung down on both sides of her. She then made the gentlemen go on one side and the ladies on the other, and each take hold of one end of a ribbon, the rule being, that those who found themselves thus united were partners, and must dance the first dance together.

"Make aunt take a ribbon," said Clara, and, much against her inclination, the good señora was obliged to yield to the supplications of the merry throng around her.

"Sky blue!" whispered Clara to Carlos, as she observed Elia making choice of this color.

Carlos followed her counsel, and, when Clara let fall the ribbons, found himself united to his lady-love. Clara looked at him and smiled significantly; but the smile left her face as she observed her aunt's look of horror upon finding herself, by a fatal casualty, joined to the Pole. Such was the anger of the Asistenta, that, placing the ribbon in Clara's hands, she exclaimed:

"You must dance with my partner, and tell him that I neither dance nor speak French. You will be delighted to dance with him, no doubt, since you speak of this son of Poland as a true Spanish woman would speak of a descendant of Pelayo." So saying, she turned her back and ran to Maria, whom she saw looking in at a door, with a face sour enough to turn all the wine in her vaults into vinegar.

"Be quick, Maria," said she. "Send for ices, jellies, cakes, chocolate, coffee, preserves, confections, wine, lemonade. Call Pedro. See that nothing is wanting."

"The countess has ordered every thing, as if she were in her own house," growled Maria.

"And why shouldn't she, woman? Are we in Lent, you grumbler, you?"

"The mats will be ruined, señora."

"Then we will buy new ones," cried the señora, running over to the other side of the room, where sat the Baroness de Bruno.

"My dear Isabel," said the baroness, "your house is a perfect bear-garden."

"I know it, baroness, but what can I do? This Clara would raise a riot in a nunnery!"

"What a looking set!" continued the baroness. "That fellow who is talking with your friend Delgado is a music-teacher. The one whose arm Clara has is a petty trader; and as for the big-whiskered rascal that she danced with, why—well, never mind what he is, but be sure to tell Maria to look out for your silver candlesticks."

"Come, come, baroness, you know he is not so bad as that, though he has had the misfortune to come from Poland." So saying, the Asistenta moved away from her as unceremoniously as she had left Maria, and approached a table where her sister-in-law was playing cards.

"How are you getting on, Ines?" she asked.

"Very well, Isabel; but I must be going, for it is getting late, and I have the headache."

"Leave Esperanza, then, sister."

"Pardon me, Isabel, but I must take her with me; for I do not allow her to dance with any but her equals, and you must admit that Clara has gathered together a very promiscuous company, to say the least of it. Good-night."

After Elia had danced the first country dance with Carlos, her hand was claimed by young Riosecco, who could not conceal the profound impression which her beauty had made upon him. Carlos seated himself near the door, and watched the beautiful pair with anxious looks. When the dance was finished, Elia took a seat near him; but Carlos, in a fit of jealousy, left the room and commenced pacing violently up and down the hall. Scarcely had Elia noted his absence, however, before he was at her side.

"Elia," said he, "do you know what the color of the ribbon which united us to-night is emblematical of?"

"Yes; the purity of Mary."

"In the language of the world, Elia, it signifies jealousy. Do you know what that is?"

"Yes, Carlos, it is the pang one feels at being deceived. San José was unjustly jealous of Mary, and so the—"

"Merciful Father, Elia!" interrupted Carlos, "do remember that you are not now in a convent—jealousy is not founded on convictions. It is this that I feel when I observe that another wishes to take my love from me, and that she forgets—"

"Do you suppose that I could forget you, Carlos?" interrupted Elia.

"At least, you did not think of me!"

"All the time, Carlos!"

"I don't believe it!"

"Since I have consented to keep silence," answered Elia, sorrowfully, "you think me capable of telling a falsehood, Carlos?"

"But didn't I see that, as soon as the music commenced, you thought of nothing but dancing and amusing yourself."

"As soon as the music commenced, Carlos, my heart sang such sweet words, in an idiom that the lips cannot pronounce! your name alone I heard distinctly."

"Many times, Elia?"

"So many, so many! may God send as many angels to me in the hour of death! So, Carlos, I cannot conceive of your being jealous, and—"

"But, Elia," said Carlos, interrupting her, "if you saw me paying attention to another, would you not be jealous!"

"No," answered Elia, "no! I should never suppose you loved me less on that account. I could never suspect you of wishing to deceive me."

"But I, who have not your admirable *sang froid*," exclaimed Carlos, getting angry again; "I, who am jealous even of the breeze which fans your cheek, do not wish you to dance with any one."

"I will not dance, Carlos."

"Nor speak to any one, Elia?"

"I will not speak, Carlos."

"I do not wish you ever to look at any one," continued Carlos, getting more exacting, as Elia became more submissive; and converting into despotism the anger which he could not vent in a quarrel.

"I will not look at any one without your consent," replied Elia, lowering her eyes.

"But why do you cry?" said Carlos, after a short silence, observing great tears trickling down her cheeks.

"I weep," replied Elia, sorrowfully, "because I find that, without knowing it, I have displeased you, and because I never thought any one would chide so harshly, and you least of all."

"Oh, pardon me, pardon me, Elia," said Carlos, vanquished by her tears, "I have been unjust, cruel; I should have remembered that the mortal who loves you can never make you descend to his sphere, but must endeavor to elevate himself to yours."

CHAPTER XIII.

CARLOS was so madly in love, and Elia so frank and sincere, that their mutual passion soon became evident to all the world save the blind Asistenta, and gave rise to the usual amount of small talk pertaining to such matters. Their mothers were, of course, "wondered at;" Carlos censured, and the "presumptuous Elia" abused beyond measure, especially by maiden ladies on the shady side of thirty. Each one traced, with admirable judgment, the line of conduct Elia should pursue and the measures she should adopt for the future; each one, in short, being, according to custom—as you are who read this, and I who write it—wise, prudent, and far-seeing in the affairs of other people.

Among those who talked most on this occasion was the Baroness of Bruno, who, as we have seen, was one of those unfortunates that, like the hedgehog, are hostile to all with whom they come in contact ; who make stilts of criticism for their own elevation, unhappily forgetful of the fact that these very stilts make every defect they themselves may happen to possess more strikingly apparent. These people—scouts for envy, telegraphs for malice—unlike the bee, which extracts from all things honey, seem to have received the sad mission of extracting poison even from honey itself. And how can this capital defect of our epoch be corrected, what check can be given to this general depreciation of men and things? Making ourselves virtuous; for with virtue there will enter into our hearts benevolence, and indulgence for the faults of others.

The baroness, then, as we said, gave a loose rein to her tongue, saying among other things that "she could not comprehend the passive conduct of the marchioness, one of the Cordobas *de la Cepa*, and as ridiculously vain as a certain female ancestor of hers, who upon hearing a bell tolling at the death of a Queen of Spain, which, ordinarily, only tolled for those of the house of Cepa, asked haughtily, 'was the queen one of the great Cordobas of Cepa, that our bell tolls for her?'"

To tell the truth, the baroness owed the marchioness a grudge, for the following reason: Her family was of somewhat recent origin; so that her family mansion, which was really magnificent, was built in much better taste than that of the marchioness, which was constructed before the conquest, and, besides being a most unsightly pile, was in a most inaccessible part of the country; for the ancient grandees isolated themselves as if they feared they might want space to stretch their powerful arms, and raised their roofs to heaven that they might not have to bend their haughty heads. So the baroness said, on a certain occasion, that "the marchioness's house was like a coarse cloak, covered with patches and *placed in a garret.*" Of course, there was not wanting a *run-see-and-tell-her*, swifter than a locomotive and more diligent than a carrier-pigeon, to report this to the marchioness, who replied, in her usual calm way, "that no one could be a better judge of these matters than the baroness, whose house was so new, that she herself might almost be considered the architect of it; and that it was certainly a pity that a new house could not accompany an old title."

We have not been able to learn whether, as a Christian woman, the lady of the new house was enabled to forgive the lady of the old one, up to the hour of her death.

The marchioness, however, notwithstanding her apparent indifference, was not a tranquil spectator of what was passing in her family; for, although she believed it an easy thing to pluck out by the roots from Carlos's heart the mad passion he had conceived for Elia, when the proper time came to speak to him on the subject, yet she feared lest his impetuous character should cause him to reveal it to the world, and thus give rise to a scandal which might be fatal to the innocent girl, whose good name she respected as much as she did her child's.

She determined at length that there was no longer any time to lose, and that Carlos must either be persuaded to renounce Elia entirely, or else forced to return to his regiment at Cadiz; and, her resolution being once taken, she became tranquil, for she thought, and she thought wisely, that there is no love which can resist reason, time, and absence united.

On his part, Carlos had long since determined to come to an understanding with his mother; but had deferred it from day to day, awaiting a favorable opportunity.

He had not sought an intermedium, because he knew that no one had any influence over his mother in family affairs, except his aunt, whom his delicacy forbade his mixing up in the matter.

One day, then, after they had finished breakfast, and the servants had retired, the marchioness, turning suddenly toward her son, said to him in a low but firm tone:

"Carlos, although it may be contrary to the maternal dignity to interfere in the gallantries of one's sons, I find it impossible to refrain from so doing on this present occasion. It is my duty as a mother to anticipate and avert the results of your follies, which you, with your impulsive character, cannot foresee. I am, therefore, under the painful necessity of prescribing to you your future course, since the past has given rise to rumors which may compromise an amiable young girl."

Upon hearing this unexpected exordium, the

brothers and sister were surprised and overwhelmed.

Fernando, knowing the character of his mother and the intentions of his brother, foresaw a violent scene, the result of which would not be what the marchioness expected; and so he said to her, "Mother, we men understand these matters better than women, and if you will permit me to make your wishes known to Carlos, a discussion painful to both may be avoided."

"No," answered the marchioness; "the counsels of a mother, to have their full force, must proceed from her own lips; from her mouth alone has her will its full authority."

Esperanza, pale and trembling, gazed nervously at her mother. Fernando seated himself in an agitated manner, and leaned his head on his hand. Carlos thought of Elia, and, wiping the perspiration from his forehead, became calm upon repeating to himself, "Now or never!"

The marchioness attributed the visible emotion of her children to their surprise at finding her acquainted with Carlos's love-affair, and thinking she would the more readily, on that account, obtain her end, continued slowly and dispassionately: "It is not my intention, Carlos, to chide you for having placed your eyes on a girl, who, as an orphan and a *protégée* of your aunt, should have been held sacred; for your reason will demonstrate it to you better than my words, and your conscience, when you listen to it, more clearly than either. The fair fame of Elia has suffered from your inconsiderate gallantry: and unblemished reputation, Carlos, is the first dowry that a man asks of a woman whom he makes his wife—the most beautiful recompense she can offer her parents—the most glorious inheritance she can bequeath to her children. It is her crown in the world, her epitaph in the tomb; and it is a flower, Carlos, that is withered by a glance. It is necessary, then, that Elia should be protected from the withering stare of the world; to effect which there is but one way —it is easy, simple, does not attract attention, and, above all, it is my *will*. Carlos, you must leave Seville without a moment's delay."

There reigned a moment of silence; upon Esperanza's clasped hands fell two large tears.

At length, Carlos, with the deference inspired by his profound respect for his mother, but with the determination and firmness which his vehement love for Elia gave him, replied:

"Mother, if you exact it, I will depart. But do not think, because I obey you in this, that I renounce my consecrated love. No, it is my life, my soul, my destiny, my whole being! I love an angel whom God has placed upon the earth to see if men would know how to appreciate her. She has accepted my love, and no power on earth can separate us!"

Such was the surprise of the marchioness, upon hearing these words, that she became dumb for the moment, and fixed her astonished and glaring eyes on her son, while a mortal pallor overspread her features.

"What!" cried she at length in a choking voice, "have my ears heard aright? Have you dared to say, in my presence, that nothing on earth can deter you from an insensate madness? Is it my son, the son of the man whom I love and revere in the grave, who has uttered these words?"

"Yes, mother, yes! it is your son, who is ready to sacrifice every thing for you except his affection. Oh mother, mother, do not condemn me! Why should you condemn a sentiment so pure, so noble, so unconquerable? Do not force me to rebel against your authority, which I have ever cheerfully submitted to—against your judgment, which I have been hitherto accustomed to consult with the confidence of the shepherd in the stars that cannot lead astray. Consent, then, dear mother, so that, receiving my wife from your hands, she may be doubly sacred!"

"And dare you even to think for a moment," exclaimed the marchioness, beside herself with passion, "of uniting yourself to a— yes! the veil must fall that, like a cloud charged with lightnings and tempests, has heretofore covered the fatal secret of her birth!— know, then—"

"Oh mother!" said Carlos, interrupting her, "what do I care? Would she make me any happier, should I love her more dearly, if she were the daughter of a king? Of what importance is it to me to know the origin of the flowers in whose bosom the honey was created which is to sweeten my life? Pride alone would hold rank in greater estimation than virtue, innocence, and beauty!"

"He is mad!" gasped the marchioness. "He neither listens to reason, nor hearkens to the voice of his mother. Come to your senses, oh my son, and leave fables to fools and children!"

"Dear mother," replied Carlos, "let me beseech you not to be as inexorable in your opposition as I am firm in my resolve. Command the *possible* that I may obey you, and do not destroy the authority which I venerate, against the rock of impossibility."

"Fly from my sight, rebellious son!" exclaimed the marchioness, tremulous with indignation. "Let not to-morrow's sun find you here! Do not appear in my presence again until you have regained your reason, and, with it, the sense of your duty to your family, and the respect which you owe to your mother."

"I will go," said Carlos, rising, "I will go, but not before renewing in your presence the oath I have sworn to Elia before Heaven. Elia, whom I love, and who loves me—Elia in whom I confide, and who confides in me—Elia shall be my wife!"

The marchioness drew herself up to her full

height, and, with a face as white as the wall, shook her finger at her child, while from her trembling lips came these terrible words:

"Then take to her as a dowry, unworthy son, the bitter curse of your mother!"

Esperanza shrieked. Fernando bent toward his brother who fell fainting in his arms.

The marchioness went out with hurried steps. Esperanza followed her to her bedroom, wringing her hands.

"Mother, mother! where are you going?" she exclaimed, as she observed her putting on her mantilla.

"I am going," answered the marchioness, "to undeceive the presumptuous girl who has dared to receive your brother's vows, and foment madness—I am going to dissipate her wild illusions."

"Oh, mother!" remonstrated Esperanza, falling on her knees before her and seizing her by the dress, "Elia is sick. Let me go to her. Let a friend open her eyes, if you persist in it, but do not go yourself—do not go yourself! at this moment, at least, do not go, I implore you!"

"Leave me," answered the marchioness, furiously, and tearing herself from her grasp as she spoke, "let me not find an adversary in each of my children!" So saying, she went forth; and Esperanza, overpowered with grief, remained kneeling, with her hands extended toward the door through which the marchioness had made her exit.

CHAPTER XIV.

Elia was somewhat indisposed, and lying on a sofa. Maria had dressed her, and standing beside her, with a spoon in one hand and a cup in the other, said to her:

"Come, Elia, take some more of this jelly; I made it and I am sure it is good."

"I will take it," answered Elia, "but it is not good if you did make it, you vain woman, you!"

"How your skin burns!" said Maria, feeling her pulse.

"You are determined to have me sick, I see," answered Elia, "and all for the purpose of making me swallow your mixtures. Take them yourself, for I am well and happier than the queen, because, to-morrow or next day, my secret will be brought to light, and then from pure content you will not sleep for three nights, nor grumble for three days."

"I'll bet," said Maria, smiling inwardly, "that this secret you talk so much of will prove to be the mountain which brought forth a mouse."

"On the contrary," returned Elia, earnestly, "it is the mouse which is about to bring forth a mountain—you will see, you will see!"

The door opened suddenly, and the marchioness, pallid, severe, and imposing, appeared before them.

The spoon dropped from Elia's hands, and Maria let fall the cup on the floor.

"Maria, leave us," said the marchioness; "I have something to say to Elia."

Maria, without moving, cast a look of unfathomable tenderness upon the agitated Elia.

"Did you hear me?" asked the marchioness, in a peremptory manner.

After waiting a moment, Maria, frightened and confused, retired. "Can it be possible?" she murmured. "No, no, it is not that, it cannot be! If she were even to allude to it, she ought to be hung up by the tongue."

When Maria had closed the door, the marchioness took a chair, and seated herself near Elia.

"Elia," said she, "there are certain matters in this world which may be hidden so long as this concealment does not give rise to great evils; but which must be revealed when there is no other way of preventing these evils. Such is the case with respect to the secret of your birth, which I now find myself under the necessity of disclosing to you."

She was silent for a moment, and then continued: "Listen to me attentively, and let what I am about to tell you serve for your guidance in the future.

"On a certain occasion, my sister and myself, on our way to one of her country-seats, drew up at the door of the inn in the village of Italia, where we saw the curate of the place, whom we both knew very well, about setting out for Seville. Isabel wished to know what urgent business carried him to Seville, where the plague was raging fearfully. We retired to a room, and the curate spoke thus:

"'A month ago, I was awakened, about midnight, by a loud rap at my door. I arose and opened it; and a man, who hid his face in a blanket, thrown over his shoulders, told me that a woman required my ministry, and requested me to go with him to her residence. I hesitated at first, in the presence of that imposing apparition, but said, finally, "Lead the way, and I will follow you." We traversed the dark and lonely streets of the village, until we came to its western outskirt, where we found two horses tied to a tree. "Where are we going?" I asked. "Where you are needed," was the curt reply. I saw that I was to be a part or perhaps a victim of some sad mystery, but I commended myself to God, and, mounting the animal designed for me, followed my guide. We had ridden, at full speed, a half hour, when he drew up at the entrance of a dense wood, and, throwing himself from his horse, motioned me to do the same. He now led the way, by a narrow path, until we came to an open space, where a bright fire was burning, around which eight or ten men were reclining: it was not easy to deceive one's self; they were robbers. "Father," said one of them to me, a young man of fine appearance, who seemed to be the leader of the gang, judging from his lofty air and tone of command, "confess this woman." He pointed, as he spoke, to an unfortunate stretched upon a blanket at his feet, and then withdrew with his companions to a little distance. I thought they were about to assassinate her, and my blood froze in my veins. I drew near to her, and, seeing she did not move, raised her head; the light of the fire fell full upon her face; it was beautiful. "Father," she cried, "I feel that I have not long to live, but before I die I desire to confess my sins, which are without number. Say, father, say, can so great a sinner die in peace—will God grant this grace to her who asks it when there is no longer any thing else for her to ask?" I calmed that agitated spirit as best I could, and found, as the unhappy woman redoubled her cries, that she was in the pangs of childbirth. It was necessary that she should have temporal succor without delay. I called the captain, and telling him of the great danger the patient was in, proposed to take her to my house, where my sister would render the aid which was indispensable. After some hesitation, he accepted my offer, upon the condition that I would give her to him again when she got well. This I promised to do, provided she should desire to go with him, which he seemed not to doubt for an instant. She was carried then to my house, where, after much suffering, she gave birth to a child, and died, resigning her soul to the Saviour's care, washed in the tears of contrition. When he, who had intrusted her to my care, came for her, I carried him to her bier. He stood a long time, silently contemplating those lovely features, which death had whitened and composed, as it purifies and tranquillizes the souls of those who die as Christians. Thus there were found, on either side of the coffin of that beautiful being, whose honor had fallen a sacrifice to love, the man who had ruined her, and the priest whose holy mission it was to save her: the one, full of terror, looking upon that death as a frightful punishment; the other, considering it as a merciful dispensation, and calmly praying to God, while, full of hope and faith, he gazed upon the corpse. I brought the babe, but upon beholding it the bandit uttered an imprecation, as if he were reproving it for causing the death of its mother, covered his face with his hands, and rushed from the house.'"

"'And abandoned it!" cried Elia, who with her hands clasped, and all her soul in her beautiful eyes, listened to the marchioness without being able to comprehend how the secret of her birth could be connected with the story she was so solemnly narrating. "Poor babe, poor forsaken one!" she continued, murmuring to herself, as the marchioness, without replying to her, proceeded:

"'I waited until now,' continued the curate, 'to see whether the father would return to claim his child, to whom I have given the name of its mother; and, as he has not made his appearance, I am about to place her in the orphan asylum at Seville.'

"'Which is the purgatory of the angels who there expiate the crimes of their parents,' cried my sister, with her usual impetuosity. 'Bring her to me, I beg of you, that I may look at her.'" They brought her asleep; but as soon as Isabel took her she opened her eyes and seemed to be looking into hers. Isabel, who always allows herself to be carried away by her first impulses, kissed her and said: 'Sir curate, this child is mine.' That child," added the marchioness, rising, "is yourself. And now consider whether the daughter of a bandit and an abandoned woman can expect to ally herself to the two first houses of Andalusia!"

Saying this, the marchioness departed, assuming a calmness which a mortal pallor and an involuntary tremor showed was not real.

Maria, who was not far off, saw her go out, and hastened to return to Elia's room, whither her cries attracted the whole household, when, upon entering it, she found the child she had nursed lying senseless on the floor, like a corpse.

With hasty steps, supported by Don Benigno, came the Asistenta.

"What is this?" she asked of the servants crowded around Elia. "What has happened?"

"She is dying, she is dying!" shrieked Maria, who had lost her presence of mind.

"Elia, Elia! child of my heart!" exclaimed the Asistenta, "a doctor! a doctor! run—fly all of you!"

Don Benigno ran to open the window; Pedro to get vinegar.

"But Maria, have you lost your senses?" said the Asistenta. "Speak! say; what produced this?"

"I do not know," answered Maria, "I was not here."

"Where were you, then, careless woman, when I trusted her to your care in her sickness, which I believed slight."

"Señora, the marchioness commanded me to leave her."

"Has my sister been here, then?" inquired the surprised Asistenta.

At this moment, Elia, who had been placed upon a sofa, opened her eyes, which she had scarcely fixed on the anxious countenance of the Asistenta, when, rising with a sudden impulse, she threw herself at her feet, and, embracing her knees, exclaimed:

"Señora, señora, I am not the daughter of a friend of yours. I am the despised child of a bandit—of a father who abandoned me! I am not worthy of the sweet name of daughter, which you have bestowed upon me; call me slave, señora! I will serve your servants, if they disdain not my service! I will put myself in my place, and it will cost me little if of all your favors you leave me that which I most appreciate, most value—your affection!"

Her sobs would not suffer her to proceed. The Señora of Calatrava had thrown herself into an easy-chair, pale as death and trembling like an aspen; and an expression of the most violent anger took the place of the dolorous surprise which had been painted on her frank and expressive countenance.

"This is an iniquity!" she murmured—"a vile treachery!—this is to have the heart of a tiger. Rise, my daughter," said she, pressing Elia to her heart, "this is your place, and will ever be it. You are my daughter, and whoever is not willing to recognize you as such, must leave my house and renounce my friendship. I will avenge you, my darling! They wish to abase you; I will raise you up—my child, my child!"

But Elia did not answer; she had fallen into a new fainting-fit, accompanied by delirium.

"Señora, señora," cried Maria, crazy with grief, "they have killed her! this is an assassination! The child was already ill, and this has opened her grave. What crime had she been guilty of, this rose without a thorn?" and Maria burst into a flood of tears.

"Maria, don't add to our lady's affliction," said Don Benigno, without withdrawing his eyes from the Asistenta's altered and mournful face.

"Console her yourself, if you can!" answered Maria.

"Pedro now entered with the doctor, who, after bleeding Elia, and putting her to bed, took his leave, promising to return in a few hours. After he had left, the Asistenta made signs to Don Benigno to follow her, and went to the library.

"Bring the inkstand," said she, after she had seated herself, with the clear voice and brevity which were natural to her when she was greatly excited.

Don Benigno was so confused at hearing these words, and the presage of what was about to happen, that, instead of an inkstand, he brought a candlestick.

"What are you thinking of, man of God?" asked the Asistenta, angrily, rising herself and bringing the inkstand with the agility of a young girl. When all was ready, she said:

"Write what I dictate."

"'You have murdered my Elia!'"

Don Benigno stopped, and his pen trembled as if it were shaken by the wind.

"Why do you not write?" asked the señora.

"Because I do not know to whom to direct the letter," said the secretary, who found it impossible to begin an epistle without heading it with the name of the person to whom it was to be sent.

"The superscription will tell you," replied the Asistenta, impatiently.

"'*Elia*,'" repeated Don Benigno after finishing the sentence.

"'You have behaved treacherously,'" continued the Asistenta. "You have offended me irreconcilably. The cruelty of your conduct toward my daughter'—(underscore the word 'daughter,' Don Benigno): *toward my daughter* have you done it!'"

"Yes, señora," replied the secretary, sorrowfully.

The Asistenta continued:

"'And your offensive and inexplicable conduct toward me induce me to inform you that you and your children may renounce forever—you, my friendship—they, my property!'"

Up to the word *friendship* inclusive, Don Benigno wrote, as well as he was able; but when he came to *property*, his pen fell from his hands; and he begged the señora, with an earnestness never before known in him, either to retract that last sentence or exempt him from the task of writing it—a task it was impossible for him to fulfil.

The Asistenta snatched the paper from his hands, made two great blots, wrote in large characters the objectionable word, signed the letter, folded it as God willed, sealed it with a large red seal, directed it, and sent it to her sister-in-law.

A half hour afterward she received a neatly-folded note. It read thus:

"The houses of Orrea and Cordoba have lived ages in opulence and honor, without having need of your property. Therefore we are all indifferent to it, leaving the thirst of gold to the lower classes; it is far different, however, with your friendship, which I regret to lose. I have taken a step, harsh perhaps, but necessary —for great evils, great remedies! But I will not condescend to excuse myself, since I do not recognize any other judge, in this matter, than my own conscience.

"Your servant, who kisses your hands,

"INES DE CORDOBA."

"And she calls my petting this angel and treating her as my child *great evils*," cried the Asistenta, indignantly, after she had read the note. "Who would believe it? But my child she shall be, let Ines fret as she may."

From which remark, it is easy to see that the good señora was a thousand leagues from suspecting the plot of that drama whose effects she felt without divining its cause.

CHAPTER XV.

AFTER the marchioness had left her, Esperanza called Fernando, and told him, sobbing, of the determination their mother had come to in her concentrated anger. She begged him to go for Father Salvador, of the order of the Capuchins, the marchioness's confessor, and the only one who exercised any influence over her haughty spirit, so jealous of her authority as a mother. This authority had always been respected by her children, in consequence of her austerity as a widow, her nobility and dignity as a woman, her entire consecration of herself to the interests of her children as a mother, and her virtues as a Christian.

"Only her confessor," said Esperanza to her brother, "only his voice, which is that of religion, can calm this tempest of the soul, as the Saviour calmed the waves of the sea."

Fernando approved of his sister's judgment, and, to avoid all publicity, instead of sending a servant, went himself to the convent, whence he presently returned with the priest.

So venerable was the appearance of the pious man, in his coarse sack and with his silvery beard, that all who looked upon him recognized the fact that it is not in gold and purple that the dignity of man shines the most resplendent.

When the marchioness returned, Father Salvador was already aware that upon that virtuous and peaceful home the maternal anathema had fallen, like a thunderbolt, leaving its scathing mark, and shaking the house to its foundation.

Upon beholding her confessor, the exasperated mother cast a glance of indignant reproof at her children, and made a sign with her hand to them to leave the room; then turning to the Capuchin, she said, with asperity: "You were sent for, I presume?"

"And if it were so?"

"I shall regard it as a piece of unparalleled insolence in my children, to wish to impose a judge upon me."

"I do not come as a judge, I come as a mediator."

"And do you expect to persuade me to give my consent to the monstrous marriage which my son desires to make?"

"You know, señora, that I have never interfered in the temporal affairs of your house. My visits are altogether spiritual."

"I trust you have at least been informed, father, of the enormity of my son's conduct, of his scandalous designs, of his impertinent emancipation. I always feared, from his want of judgment, that he would fall into grave errors; but I never imagined that, at the age of twenty-two, he would endeavor to dishonor his family, stain his escutcheon, defy public opinion, and tread under foot the will of his mother—no, I never imagined any thing half so horrible!"

"Your youth so happily passed in the retirement of the convent," answered Father Salvador, "your even temperament, your happy marriage have preserved you from the violence of the passions; therefore you know nothing of them, and judge too hastily and harshly of their effects upon your son."

"Do you mean to excuse filial disobedience and madness?"

"By no means. I will only warn you, marchioness, that passion is never more absolute and decided than when confronted by despotic obstacles, never more arrogant than when it finds itself despised. Sweetness of temper and prudence effect more, in time, than rigor and intolerance."

"And is it a minister of religion, a judge in the confessional," asked the marchioness, with bitter irony, "who counsels indulgence toward the passions?"

"It is because I am such, señora, that I give this counsel—otherwise who would kneel at our feet? Marchioness," added the director, in a composed but firm voice, "you are right in what you condemn and prohibit; and so your will shall be obeyed, and your son depart: you cannot and should not exact more. But you have acted with violence and pride, and you must retract your maternal curse, so lightly and irreligiously given."

"I! I!" exclaimed the marchioness, while the flush of anger overspread her pallid features,

"*I* retract one moment what I have said the moment before? *I* humble myself before my children? *I* yield to an insensate rebel? You are jesting, father. I thought you knew, ere now, that fickleness is not one of my failings."

"But it will, on this occasion, be a virtue of which you can boast. I have often told you, marchioness, that humility—this despised virtue which, like the unpolished diamond, neither shines nor sparkles—is the most reliable guide to perfection."

"If humility require a mother to humble herself before a son given up to his unblinded passions, if it require her to lend him wings, instead of placing fetters upon him, to fly to a precipice—sir, a good mother renounces this *virtue!*"

"While you continue, then, in this frame of mind," said Father Salvador, rising, "you cannot, under my direction, partake of the holy sacraments."

"Ah, well!" replied the marchioness, with angry haughtiness, "ah, well! there are other priests in Seville who will look at this matter from another point of view, and who will not exact from me that which compromises my dignity. Let the cause cease, and its effects will cease. Preach this doctrine of humility to the son, in whom it would be more becoming than in the mother."

"You know I am not the director of his conscience, señora."

"Neither can you be of mine, hereafter. I will not give this rebellious son such an advantage over me."

"Then my functions here cease," answered the confessor, calmly. "Our yoke is so voluntary that it can be shaken off at pleasure. What comes from God, comes accompanied with free will, without which vice would not be culpable, nor virtue entitled to its reward. For myself," added the upright counsellor, "I cannot depart from what appears my duty as your spiritual director. Adieu, señora; remember that, if I do not yield, it is because I ought not, and my conscience will not permit me to do so, but that obstinacy alone hinders you from yielding."

Saying this, he went out with a slow step, and when the last fold of the coarse habit of the Capuchin disappeared through the crack of the door, a choking voice was heard:

"Father Salvador! Father Salvador, return! I obey you!"

The religious woman had triumphed over her passions; the Catholic stood upon the head of the serpent. The marchioness had let her stately head fall upon her hands, and a torrent of tears streamed from her eyes.

"Daughter," said the father, reëntering the room, in a voice profoundly moved, "there is more merit in this than in a year of ascetic life."

On the following day, Carlos, absolved, left Seville, sacrificing with the most violent grief his present happiness, but firm in his hopes for the *future*.

CHAPTER XVI.

One month after the events narrated in our last chapter, a profound silence reigned in Elia's chamber, which, but a little before, was the sanctuary of flowers, songs, and happiness. The window-curtains were carefully drawn, to exclude the light. The perfume of the jasmin and tuberose had given place to the smell of lavender and burnt sugar; pomades, ribbons, and flowers were replaced on the toilet-table by jellies, pills, and prescriptions. The Virgin of Hope, whose altar was under the immediate care of the Asistenta, and San Antonio, the favorite saint of Maria, were hanging at the head of the bed. On the bureau was a crucifix, with a blessed candle burning before it. Peeping out from under the pillows of a bed, as white as a lily, were the silken cords of a little bag containing precious relics which had been sent by the nuns. In short, all that Catholic apparatus was seen there which unbelievers behold without being able to comprehend that it gives courage in danger, supports in grief, and robs death of its terrors.

At the head of the bed sat the Asistenta, and at the foot Don Benigno, whose anxious eyes wandered alternately from the bed to his mistress, whose sunken cheeks showed the effects of care and watchfulness. Near her was Maria, seated on a low chair, and holding in her hand a fly-brush, with which she waged perpetual war upon the flies that dared to invade the sacred spot where Elia, her darling, was reposing.

Elia lay immovable upon the bed; the bloom of youth and health had disappeared from her cheek, and, at a little distance, the sleeping girl might have been confounded with the white sheets, had it not been for her dark hair, which, parted in the middle, hung down on both sides of her pallid face—seeming, to a superstitious mind, like the black hands of Death, claiming that inert head as their prey.

The group we have described was full of

profound interest, and made a picture just the opposite of that which we are accustomed to imagine for our consolation; for, in this case, instead of the compassionate angels watching over the miseries of humanity, these were watching over an angel: the Asistenta, personating old age, Don Benigno impotency, and Maria, who was worn to a skeleton, from grief and watching, sickness and sorrow, with their attendant evils.

"This is the longest and most quiet sleep she has had," said the Asistenta, softly.

"By far," answered Don Benigno, pulling out his immense watch—"forty-three minutes and a half."

"And this is San Antonio's day!" exclaimed Maria, opening her hands and extending them toward the image of the saint with an expression of fervent gratitude.

After a little while, the Asistenta said, as if she were following out the thread of her previous reflections:

"Carlos has gone, so I hear, and has not come to bid me good-by—nor my poor child, whom he appeared to be so fond of—nor even you, Don Benigno, who were so patient with him. Who would have believed it? I never see any one now but Fernando, who makes a lame excuse for his brother, by saying that he went off in a great hurry. And this sister-in-law of mine, more cruel than King Don Pedro, after putting my child at death's door, not to come near her, nor even to send a message to inquire after her! If you can find an excuse for such conduct, Don Benigno—how much better the name suits you than your baptismal one of Zacharias!—if you can find an excuse for such conduct as this, I repeat, Don Benignissimo, as Carlos calls you, you are capable of raising an altar with this inscription:

'To the Great and Good Herod.'"

At this moment, Elia opened her beautiful eyes, and fixed them with an indescribable expression of sweetness and gratitude on the persons who surrounded her. Don Benigno rose hurriedly, and, knocking down every thing within his reach in his great effort to move noiselessly, went to draw closer one corner of a curtain which admitted a ray of light.

Maria smoothed the sheets, and the Asistenta took the patient's hand, and, after feeling her pulse, placed her cheek upon her forehead.

"How shall I ever repay so much kindness?" said Elia, in a feeble voice. "One single heart is not enough; a lifetime is too short!"

"Silence," answered the Asistenta, placing her hand over Elia's mouth, "silence, you little goose! It is for us to thank you that you are improving so fast, taking your medicine like a good child as you are. For, my darling, if you were wanting, would there be sunlight in the house, flowers in the garden, or consolation for us? Now, my heart," she added, after a few minutes' silence, "I am going to the cathedral to hear the mass I vowed to the Virgin of Kings if she would heal you. It is now ten o'clock, and the mass begins at eleven. Good-by, my darling. Maria, tell her a story, and do your best to amuse her until I return."

When the Asistenta had departed, accompanied by Don Benigno, Elia and her nurse found themselves alone for the first time since the visit of the marchioness. Elia gazed for a long time in Maria's eyes, and, in the soft languor of her glance, there was a supplication her lips dared not utter, even in the presence of this loved and trusted attendant.

The quick-witted Maria at once understood this mute question, she had expected and feared; for she did not wish Elia to know of Carlos's departure, which she highly disapproved; and yet she dreaded her hearing it from the Asistenta, who constantly spoke of her nephews. To be apprised of it suddenly by the señora, without being prepared for it, might give her a great shock, and make her ill again; so she took an indirect method of giving the wound and its balsam at the same time.

"I am going," said she, "to tell you a story, as the señora directed.

"There was once a young shepherdess so good and pretty, and such a perfect Christian, that she seemed an angel. Driving her flock before her, on a certain occasion, through a sterile mountain-pass, in search of pasture, she came to a plain as green and fragrant as the one we crossed on our way to Romeral. In the midst of a bed of wild flowers, which seemed to wish to bury her amid their luxuriance, she noticed an old ruin, whose thick walls appeared as sad as one who cannot live, and yet fears to die. In a part of it which was only prevented from falling by a cypress-tree growing beside it, there was a niche containing an image of our Lady; her clothes, which were wet by the rains and shaken by the winds of heaven, hanging about her in discolored rags. The little shepherdess began to weep bitterly, saying, 'Oh my mother, my mother! how lonely and deserted you are! What a sorrow! What a sin! The Queen of Heaven so neglected upon earth! Oh! that I were rich enough to repair this chapel and reëstablish your worship here, or at least buy you a garment.' And, not being able to do any thing more, she set to work to clean the niche, and hung it round with garlands which she made from the flowers of the field. And every day, while her sheep fed on the abundant pasture, she wove fresh garlands for the niche, and taught the little lambs to bend the knee before the image.

"It happened that a very handsome prince, returning one day from the chase, passed by the ruin; and no sooner had he set eyes upon the beautiful girl engaged in her pious avocation, than he fell madly in love with her, and offered her his hand. But the queen, who was prouder than Lucifer himself, did not desire a beautiful and pious shepherdess for a daughter-in-law; but a princess, even though she were as wicked as Barabbas and uglier than I am. And so, to separate him from his sweetheart, she sent him on an embassy to a neighboring kingdom. The son, who was too obedient by far, yes, *by far*," repeated Maria, laying great stress upon these words, " obeyed her orders; but he soon returned, more enamoured than before, as is always the case with true lovers, and married the shepherdess as truly and reverently as I married the schoolmaster; and the shepherdess, whom the Virgin had made rich and happy, in recompense for her devotion, repaired the chapel as she had desired to do; and so my story ends with bread, and pepper, and a grain of salt, and I've no more to say."

"No, Maria," said Elia, sadly, while the tears trickled down her sunken cheeks—for she had understood her nurse, and knew that Carlos was gone—" you have not told the story as *it is*, but as you would like it to be, and so made a *fable* of it. The truth is, the unhappy shepherdess never saw her beautiful prince again; but one night the shepherds hearing her moan piteously, went into her hut, which was in the midst of the ruins, and found her lying on the wet straw (for it was raining), with her head upon the hard ground; and seeing her so sick, they ran to a neighboring convent, whence two of the monks immediately went forth to aid her. As they drew near the hut, they observed a great light, and thought it was on fire, but when they entered it they saw a number of beautiful youths, whose white raiment shone like the sun at noonday. By the shepherdess, holding her head in her lap, sat a lovely lady, and, as the monks looked upon her with amazement, the sufferer sighed, and with a sweet smile expired. The lady then made a sign to the youths, who took the corpse in their arms, and unfolding their wings bore it to heaven; for they were angels, and the Lady the Virgin of the Ruins, who returned to her niche to gain more souls for Paradise. This is the truth, Maria. Oh, happy shepherdess, who never divided her heart, but kept it entire for God and the Virgin! I will go, my dear nurse, to some place where I can purify my soul, and prepare myself for the life to come."

Elia raised her eyes, as she spoke, and her tears ceased to flow, as if worldly tears had no place in heaven.

Maria, upon beholding such ideal beauty and such sublime holiness, turned toward the image of the Virgin, and imagined that she saw the señora casting down her eyes to meet the upward gaze of the angelic Elia.

CHAPTER XVII.

Poor Maria, whose moral energy had overcome her physical weakness, so long as Elia required nursing, now found that she had overtasked her strength, which was so completely exhausted that she was compelled to keep her bed.

Her room was on the ground-floor, directly under Elia's, and, like hers, looked out on the garden.

One day, after she began to grow stronger, she seated herself in an arm-chair, by the window, and gazed sadly upon the blue sky, in which were floating a number of fleecy clouds, as white as the driven snow, and as pure as every thing is which raises itself above the earth.

The jasmines, entwined about the bars of the window, and moved by the evening air, seemed to be tapping an invitation to her, with their white fingers, on the panes, to throw up the sash and enjoy their fragrance, with that of their neighbors, the roses, on the garden wall. The cypresses, covered with legions of birds, were converted into green towers of Babel, while the fountain, sparkling at their feet, threw its spray far up into the branches, sometimes startling the feathered songsters from their perch.

"Well, Maria," said Pedro, coming into her room with a bowl of gruel, "how goes it? As usual, I suppose—sickness going off and grumbling coming on."

"As you are always as round and sound as an apple, and have a face like the full moon," answered Maria, "what can you know of sickness? Look at my face, and you can see how ill I have been."

"And why didn't you take care of yourself? Couldn't the child have been looked after properly without your killing yourself nursing her?"

"No one could have taken my place, Pedro."

"Nonsense!" said Pedro, "you women think, in your infinite wisdom, that no one can watch over sick people but yourselves."

"And we are right, Pedro."

"Don't we all love the child with our whole hearts, Maria?"

"Every one loves her, Pedro, but no one can love her as I do who nursed her. In return for your many foolish stories, in support of your nonsensical sayings, I will tell you one in support of what I have just said:

"There was once a woman so given up to her vices, so base and avaricious, that her heart became as hard as the metal she worshipped, so that she even took her new-born infants and threw them out of a window into the river. If she ever repented of her sins, and went to confession to bewail them, she soon relapsed into vice, and became as wicked as before. Her confessor finally told her that when she was again tempted of the devil to destroy her offspring, to nurse it once before doing so. The woman promised solemnly to obey him, and she was again blessed with a child; she first nursed it, and then took it to the window to throw it out; but, Pedro, she could not; she hugged it to her breast, and, bathed in tears, became a mother and a virtuous woman."

At this moment they heard a knock at the door, and Pedro took himself off.

"Who's there?" asked Maria.

"Who do you suppose?" was the answer, in a well-known voice.

"Is it you, Catana?"

"Your servant, and no other."

"May you be God's for many years to come, Catana."

"May He ever guard you!" said the housekeeper of the marchioness, now entering.

"And you also, my friend," responded Maria, endeavoring to rise to meet her visitor.

"Sit sill, sit still," said Catana, hurrying forward, and kindly forcing her into her seat.

"The best compliment you can pay is to dispense with compliment. How ill you have been!"

"Yes, indeed, Catana, I have been on the rack by day, and in torment all night."

"It is this easterly weather."

"No, the east wind and I agree very well together."

"It is, then, that gale from the sea that blew the other day, and was as wet as the waves from which it came."

"Wrong again, Catana; the sea-breeze always kills the north wind, which is my executioner."

"What is it, then, Maria?"

"Anxiety and watching over our darling Elia, Catana, who has been ill with a fever."

It was not, however, as one might suppose from this conversation, solicitude for the health of her friend alone which brought Catana to her sick-room. She had observed, with surprise, the estrangement of the sisters-in-law, so closely united up to this time; the sudden departure of Carlos; the illness of Elia. She marked the coincidence of these events, without being able to discover the slightest thing relating to them from the austerely reserved marchioness; so she came to see if she could not get the desired information from Maria, who she felt sure had been informed of every thing by her mistress. But to get any thing out of Maria required a great deal of tact, for the discretion of the faithful servant was proverbial; so Catana began the conversation from a point of departure as distant as possible from the object she had in view.

"My dear friend," said she, "I beg of you to tell me how you make your orange pudding; for my mistress is eternally declaring that I do not make it as well as you do."

Maria was exceedingly flattered by so great a triumph over her rival: she smiled with more satisfaction than Apollo felt when he triumphed over Marsyas; but, more generous than the god, instead of flaying her competitor, she answered:

"To the juice of nine oranges, add a pound of powdered sugar, beaten up with the yolks of a dozen fresh eggs, and two tablespoonfuls of the finest flour. Place it in a tin form, well greased with lard, to prevent the pudding from sticking to it. Place the tin in an earthen pot filled with boiling water, and put the pot on live coals; and in five minutes your pudding is ready. This is the way I make it, and my señora calls it '*my child's* pudding;' but you make it as well as I do, and the marchioness does me too much honor in complimenting me at your expense. I suppose it is as the Scriptures say, however, 'a prophet has no honor in his own country.'"

Catana thanked Maria for her minute receipt, and then asked:

"Have you any thing new to tell me, Maria?"

"How could I learn any thing new here," answered Maria, "shut up as I am between four walls, like a chicken in its shell? I see no one but Pedro, and he says, in his impudent way, that to tell any thing to a woman is like telling it to the town-crier."

"I can tell you something, then," said Catana. "The countess's French cook, who gives himself more airs than a grandee of Spain, left her service the other day, because he said he found Spanish beef tough and our chickens thin. The countess added ten dollars a month to his wages, however, and he deigned to stay."

"He may go to Guinea," replied Maria; "my mistress says she cannot eat his stews, and that he doesn't even know how to roast a turkey."

"But, my friend, now that no one can hear us," said Catana, "isn't it a pity that our ladies, who have always been so intimate, should have fallen out with each other, all on a sudden?"

The physiognomy of Maria, which up to this time wore so pleasant an expression, flushed as it was by her recent triumph over her fellow-disciple of the great Soyer, changed its aspect at these words, and gradually assumed its wonted sourness.

"What has brought about this trouble," continued Catana, "is a mystery even for the oldest and most faithful of our house. I warrant the Asistenta has not been so reserved with you, and that you are not ignorant of any thing that has happened. It is really hard, after having served the marchioness so long, to find myself treated as a stranger, and not to know what to answer when I am questioned about the matter."

Maria did not open her lips for some time. At length she replied:

"Catana, if you wish to know any thing concerning myself, I will throw my heart wide open to you as a friend; but in relation to my mistress's affairs, you must pardon me if I keep silence: for my faults may be many; but I am as loyal as gold, as true as steel, and as trusty as a watch-dog."

CHAPTER XVIII.

Some time after this, the Asistenta and Elia were seated opposite to each other at a table covered with fancy-work, which the señora had bought for her child, whose profound sadness was painfully apparent, notwithstanding the effort she made to conceal it.

Elia was more beautiful than ever, because the first tears that a maiden sheds extinguish in her eyes the inquisitive stare of childhood, and inaugurate in them the soft, pensive look of womanhood.

The Asistenta was talking to Maria about Elia's recovery.

"Certainly, Maria," said she, "if we had given Elia chicken-broth, as Doctor Narciso directed, she would have died."

"He says that diet kills the disease," observed Don Benigno.

"Yes, and the patient also," replied the Asistenta. "These physicians of the new school are like the man who, wishing to kill a fly on his neighbor's forehead, gave him so violent a blow that he killed him.

"And now that you are well again, my darling, you must be as happy and gay as you used to be. How I do wish I could find something that would give you pleasure!—Ah," she continued, turning toward Don Benigno, "where is the letter that arrived for Elia when she was so sick? Now that I think of it, bring it here, for it may serve to amuse her."

Had the Asistenta not been so innocent and unsuspecting, she would have observed the embarrassment and emotion which her words produced on her hearers. All three were silent. "Have I spoken in Greek?" she asked at length.

"There was such confusion here at that time," answered Maria, who observed the blush on Elia's cheek, and the anguish expressed in her eyes, "that I am quite sure Don Benigno must have lost the letter."

"Don Benigno lose a letter!" exclaimed the Asistenta; "what nonsense you talk, woman!

One would suppose you had known him but a day. You have not lost it, I am sure, Don Benigno!"

"No, señora, I have not," he replied, too honorable and truthful to assist Maria in her stratagem.

"Then, why do you not get it?"

"Señora," answered the confused Benigno, "I fear it will not be good for the child to endeavor to make out a letter so illegibly written that I can scarcely read its superscription."

"You can read it to her as you read mine to me."

"But," said Maria, with a smile which she intended should be roguish and pleasant, but which really degenerated into a grin, "but, señora, the señorita may have her little secrets like other young girls of her age."

"Secrets! and from me!" exclaimed the Asistenta, looking at Elia with surprise; and then, observing the expression of her face, she added, "let us speak no more of it, then; you shall keep your secrets to yourself, my darling."

"No, no," exclaimed Elia, "I will not keep them to myself. They would weigh upon my conscience like a sin, and on my heart as an ingratitude.—Don Benigno," she added, "I beg you to bring the letter."

Don Benigno remained immovable, and looked at Maria, as the miller looks for the wind. Maria pulled at Elia's skirt and said, in a low voice, "Wait until he returns; you have no one to protect you now."

"Bring the letter, Don Benigno," said the Asistenta, gravely. "Elia does well not to conceal any thing from her mother, and I am surprised that one of my household should advise her to do so."

Don Benigno obeyed instantly, and returned with the letter, which he gave to Elia, who without opening it handed it to her mother.

"Do you know whom it is from?" asked the Asistenta.

"No," answered Elia, "but I suspect."

The Asistenta opened the letter and read:

"Elia:

"A despotic will, a tyrannical duty obliges

me to depart, without having the sad consolation of saying farewell—that hard word which precedes absence and death.

"Let not your heart be troubled by the events of the past few days.

"Mine you will soon be, before men and the world, as you have been before God and the angels, since the hour when, calling upon them as witnesses, I placed upon your finger the ring, symbol of eternity.

"Absence and time will only prove to you my constancy and infinite love.

"Your own CARLOS."

It is impossible to describe the varied expressions of surprise, displeasure, mortification, and grief, which passed across the countenance of the Asistenta (who never could conceal her feelings) as she read this letter.

When she had finished it, she raised her hands to heaven and then let them fall upon her knees, as she threw herself back in her armchair, exclaiming, "Jesus Maria!"

Here followed a great silence, which no one dared to break, since the señora was so absorbed in her reflections that she did not notice the heart-rending sobs of Elia.

Large tears ran down Maria's cheeks, who looked at her darling with an expression of devotion such as is rarely seen upon the earth.

Don Benigno fixed his anxious eyes upon the Asistenta.

"This was the reason, then," she said, after a long silence, and stopped short.

But Elia, who had understood her, finished the sentence. "Yes," said she, "this was the reason that the marchioness came here, as it was her duty to do, to enlighten me, and not suffer me, in my ignorance, to take advantage of her son's love and generosity; and it was a mark of kindness and delicacy in her to let the *no*, which restored things to their former state, come from her mouth instead of my lover's. So you see, she did what the noble mother of Carlos, and the generous woman who felt for me, should have done. If you only knew, my mother, how great my grief is—my remorse at seeing the noble family that I love and venerate, at variance on my account! Oh, mother! oh, señora!" she added, falling on her knees, "I beg you, as

I pray to God for glory, to become reconciled to your sister. Let me not be like the serpent which the generous woodman sheltered, and infuse, like it, venom into the bosom which shelters me! Let your heart do justice to the worthy mother who watches over the honor of her house and race, as she formerly watched beside the cradle of her children, driving away the perils not seen by eyes then closed in sleep, but now blinded by passion. Pardon her just dread and suspicion! If I had the reproach of sowing enmity, let me bear also the laurel of reconciliation."

"No!" answered the Asistenta. "I pardon injuries done to myself, but not those inflicted on my friends. I can excuse Ines for all except her hardness of heart. Without consulting me —against my wishes—she disclosed a secret not her own. And, after placing you on the verge of the grave, neither her heart nor her conscience has prompted her to inquire after you. This is not only an indication of pride, but of a lack of charity; and charity is the key to heaven. Rise, my child," she added, taking her by the hand, "and don't speak again on this subject, unless you wish to vex me; for the more humble and sweet-tempered you appear in my eyes, the more egotistical and hard-hearted she seems: so you will work the very opposite of what you desire."

After uttering these words, the good woman returned to her meditations, which were bitter enough. "And I never observed any thing," she said to herself; "it is unpardonable—blind! blind as the day I was born!—an Orrea, a descendant of King Pedro! It cannot be! God knows but Ines may have been right. Perhaps she would have been better off in the convent, and I have been the author of her unhappiness. Is it possible, then, that good produces evil, and excessive goodness and affection do harm?— Don Benigno," said she at length, "you who have studied, explain to me why it is that people who take prudence and reason for their guides succeed better, in their endeavors to do good to their neighbors, than those who suffer themselves to be led entirely by their affections?"

"Señora," answered Don Benigno, "in my studies, which were not extended far, I do not remember ever to have seen any thing on the subject; but to my limited understanding it seems clear that it is because the sphere of prudence is the world, and that of the heart, heaven; and we cannot, as the Evangelist says, 'serve two masters.'"

CHAPTER XIX.

THE knowledge which the Asistenta had acquired, of the mutual passion of the two beings whom she loved best on earth, had been a terrible blow to her. The thought that she might have avoided all this misfortune had she but listened to her sister's prudent counsel, and the void which she felt in her heart at being separated from all her family (for Clara had returned to England), preyed upon her mind and affected her health.

In vain did Pedro fatten turkeys with walnuts; in vain did Maria put in operation all the resources of the culinary art—the Asistenta could not eat; and, at night, the maid, who slept in the chamber adjoining hers, heard her groan in her sleep.

Fernando, who had never ceased to call daily on his aunt, whom he loved most tenderly, consulted her physician on her altered appearance, who advised immediate change of air. The weather had become warm, from the long April days, so that the Asistenta was easily persuaded to make her annual visit to the country somewhat earlier than usual, which she hoped would benefit Elia as well as herself, who was still looking thin and dejected.

The journey was undertaken, then, but not with the merriment of other days—a spring time without its flowers and birds.

They alighted at the inn in Italia, where, as in former days, the curate awaited their coming. Sad recollections did the poor inn awaken in all those who were gathered there; for here it was that the curate, seventeen years before, had brought the forsaken babe, which, without having a voice to ask assistance, had found a charity more prejudicial perhaps from its excess than the scant charity of those who practise it as a profession. There it had been snatched from its humble lot—but was this a blessing? or was it a curse? Time alone could answer.

All were wrapped in their sad meditations, when a noise was heard on the street, and the servants of the inn ran to the front door, crying out, "Castro! Castro!"

"What is the matter? who is this Castro?" asked the Asistenta.

"Is it possible, señora," answered the curate, "that you have never heard of Castro, that implacable officer intrusted with the persecution of robbers?"

"Señora," cried Maria, rushing into the room, "the soldiers have had a fight with robbers near the village, and are coming here with their wounded and prisoners. Good gracious! How dreadful! Let us be off!"

The curate rose to depart.

"Where are you going?" asked the Asistenta.

"To succor the wounded and minister to the dying," was the reply.

He went out, and Maria hastened to close the door, to hide from her mistress the terrible spectacle of which the inn was about to become the theatre.

The soldiers came in in a body, dragging along the wounded and the dying, and throwing them roughly on the stone pavement of the hall.

Women were screaming, horses neighing, and, above all the tumult, was heard the word of command of the indefatigable Castro.

"Let us go! let us go!" exclaimed the Asistenta, "since we can do no good here."

"Wait until they have entered and left the passage clear," said Maria, who was looking out of the window, and, pale and trembling, watched for an opportunity of escaping from the dreadful scene.

After a while the door opened, and the curate entered.

In his countenance, usually so calm, was depicted profound emotion. He approached the Asistenta, and, drawing her to one side, said in a low voice:

"Señora, two steps from here Elia's father is dying. He has recognized me, and asks for his daughter. Shall I be doing my duty if I deny her to him and snatch from a dying man his last consolation? Shall I hinder a child from closing the eyes of her father? May not her presence evoke the tender feelings of the sinner, and, raising his heart to heaven, prevent his dying in terrible final impenitence?"

The Asistenta was beside herself. "My poor child!" she cried, passionately. "This will kill her!—No! no! no! I cannot consent. What obligation is she under to one who dissolved every tie when he abandoned her? No, no, she must not know of this—let us depart at once."

"Señora," replied the curate, "consider that we have no right to interfere between parent and child. Tell her what has occurred, and let her decide for herself. To judge for another in so grave a matter is to assume a fearful responsibility."

The Asistenta fell upon a bench, overpowered by her emotions.

Elia ran toward her. "What is the matter, my mother? what has happened?" she asked.

"There is not a moment to lose," said the curate.—"Elia, your father is here, and is dying!"

Upon hearing these words, Elia gave a wild scream, and rushed from the room. The curate followed her; and when the Asistenta, supported by Fernando, and trembling in every limb, reached the spot where the bandit lay, she found her on her knees—divine as charity, sublime as Christian valor, beautiful as filial duty—resting on her innocent bosom a dark, bloody, terrible head, that a brave man would have shrunk from, and pressing to her pure lips a blood-stained hand whose touch would have caused loathing in a hangman.

The bandit opened his eyes, and fixed them on this celestial apparition.

"This," said the curate, "is your pure and innocent daughter, who comes to show you God's clemency and the road to heaven."

"Seraph, whom God sends me in the hour of death," said the dying man, in a feeble voice and in broken sentences—"like hope—like mercy—that I may trust in them!—pray to God for the pardon I implore! God will hear your voice, because you have heard His when He says, 'Honor thy father and mother,' and He excepts nobody."

He pressed the curate's hand—and expired.

Elia was carried to the carriage, which drove off at full speed.

"Ah!" said Maria, lavishing her cares on Elia, "what imprudence! what cruelty! what barbarity! How could the curate have been guilty of such an atrocity?"

"Maria," answered the Asistenta, one sea of tears, "let us not undertake to judge our priests. If good results from what they think it their duty to do, our censure is a rash calumny; and if they err with good intentions, our criticism is, at best, an unwarrantable impertinence. Who can say that the curate has not saved a soul?"

The curate and Castro remained alone in the parlor of the inn, where the latter had determined to await reënforcements from Seville.

The sun had set, and night was upon them with its silence.

They were seated *vis-à-vis*, at a small table, upon which a lamp was burning, whose flame was flickering as if fatigued with the impossible task of lighting all that gloomy apartment. It shone full, however, upon the white head of the curate, while the dark, curly hair of Castro was in the shade of the screen. These two figures— the man of peace and the man of action—apostles of divine and human power—formed thus a marked contrast: the one in his simple, black garb, with a rosary hanging from the waist; the other in dazzling military costume, sword by his side and pistols in his belt. The curate rose frequently to attend to the wounded, and Castro to listen to the window for the tramp of the soldiers from Seville, or the stealthy step which should announce an attempted surprise on the part of the bandits to relieve their chief, whose death they were not probably apprised of.

At length the curate said to Castro, " You lead a very fatiguing life! Don't you want to sleep a little?"

"I watch, that others may sleep," was the reply.

" But don't you desire to rest sometimes?"

" There is no rest for me," answered Castro, bitterly.

" Señor," said the curate, with a sweet smile, " this word should have a place in the mouth of reprobates only."

" Or of the despairing," added Castro.

" There is no grief without consolation in a Christian soul, Señor Castro."

" You are wrong, curate; there are sorrows which leave the soul without consolation, and with one only desire."

"And that is—"

"The thirst for revenge."

"Would that you had substituted forgiveness for revenge, Señor Castro!"

"How easy it is to pronounce this word, curate!"

"Señor Castro, when the soul *wills*, the heart *obeys*."

"And do you believe, father, that all crimes can be pardoned?"

"All, without exception."

"Tell me, then, how to forgive what I am about to narrate to you; and if you find it feasible, I will efface the word *impossible* from my vocabulary.

"On a wedding tour with my bride, whom I idolized, I was attacked by bandits, who took us prisoners after I had killed two of their number and wounded a third. Furious at this, they tied me to a tree and placed a gag in my mouth; and then beat my wife's brains out, before my eyes, with the butt-ends of their muskets. I saw her rolling at my feet, in the agonies of death. I saw her fix her dying eyes on mine, asking aid in her helpless misery. I counted her sighs and groans; I saw her die, abandoned by the universe!—and I was there—was there!—without being able to assist her, or to withdraw my sight from that dreadful picture! Her blood wet my feet, and she expired with her eyes fastened on mine, in which she read a never-dying promise of vengeance—and I live solely to fulfil it!"

At this instant the door opened, and Fernando appeared. "Captain Castro," said he, "I come to ask a favor of you."

"Do not say ask, but *demand*," answered Castro, brusquely but frankly.

"Can you dispose of these malefactors as you think proper?" continued Fernando.

The face of Castro assumed a sinister expression.

"Do you come, señor," said he, "to intercede for these villains?"

"No," answered Fernando, "I come to ask you to give me a dead body."

"The captain's, perhaps; it must not be. His head shall be placed on a post, that in death it may frighten evil-doers as in life it terrified the good.'

"You deny my request, then?"

"I must do so," answered Castro. But after a moment's silence he added: "What do you want to do with the body? Is it for a curious phrenological study?"

"No, señor," answered Fernando, "I wish to bury it."

"As a good Christian!—as an honorable man!" exclaimed Castro. "This would indeed be a bad example."

"Captain Castro," replied Fernando, "the living do not envy the prerogatives of the dead."

Castro gave some turns through the room, and then stopping before Fernando he asked abruptly, "Do you attach much value to your request?"

"An infinite value."

"Take it, then. I cannot deny any thing to the Marquis of Val-de-Jara, not on account of his rank or order, but on account of the estimation in which his character is held by all who know or have heard of him."

"Captain Castro," answered Fernando, deeply moved, "believe me, that the esteem and gratitude with which you inspire me by this favor, and your manner of granting it, will never be blotted from my memory."

When day broke, the body of the bandit had found rest and protection in the village grave-yard, and in its little church a mass for the dead was said, in solemn silence and with profound devotion.

In the obscurity of the dawn, a noble youth was discerned kneeling near the altar. This was Fernando.

CHAPTER XX.

ONE month afterward the house of the Asistenta had changed its aspect. It was no longer the smiling mansion, whose rose-tinted atmosphere seemed imbued with the spirit of welcome possessed by its mistress. There reigned in it now a gloomy silence, while throughout its wide halls were to be seen naught but trembling forms, and countenances disfigured with care and watching. On a table in the court-yard, whose gates were wide open, lay a large card of pasteboard, covered with the names of the persons who each instant called to inquire after the health of the good señora. At the head of the list was inscribed in large letters—

"The Asistenta continues dangerously ill."

In a darkened room, on a snowy couch, half concealed by the heavy folds of the curtain which hung from its massive tester, lay the patient, the only one in the house unmoved by her critical condition. On one side of the bed was Elia, on the other Maria, and at its foot knelt the worthy Don Benigno. These persons neither spoke nor wept, and scarcely seemed to respire. In an adjoining apartment three physicians were in consultation. Fernando, standing near, listened to their deliberations, pallid but serene.

"Señor marquis," said the family physician, "since her ladyship's return from the country, her illness has alarmingly increased, and is aggravated by some mental trouble which we have not been able to fathom—it is perhaps the presentiment of her approaching end. She must die."

"It is as I expected," replied the marquis, calmly. " Pedro, summon your lady's confessor." Then seating himself, he wrote these lines, which he sent by a servant to the house of the marchioness:

"Mother, aunt is about to receive extreme unction."

The confessor soon arrived, and was shown into the sick-room.

"How do you find yourself now, señora?" he asked.

"All is peace," she replied, half opening her closed eyes.

"Have you any thing more to communicate to me?" he continued.

"Nothing; my worldly affairs are arranged. But if you think me worthy of it, father, I should like to receive the last sacraments."

"Most gratifying will it be to me, my daughter," returned the priest, "to administer to you those fountains of grace and consolation."

A deep groan escaped from the breast of Elia, as, clinging to the bed-post, she resisted the gentle efforts of Fernando to remove her.

"My poor child!" sighed the Asistenta; "leave her, Fernando. I would fain have her with me in my last moments."

In the mean time, Maria, inspired by the solemnity of the ceremonial which was being prepared, had raised an altar at the foot of the bed, covered with gold and silver, and crowned with a magnificent crucifix of marble.

Notice having been sent to the relations and intimate friends of the dying woman, the house now began to be thronged with persons, whose silence and affliction testified to their tenderness and attachment; while from the spacious vestibule came the stifled sobs of the domestics and of the many poor who had subsisted upon the Asistenta's bounty.

At a little distance might be descried people with their heads uncovered, kneeling in the streets and balconies; and little children leaving their games, and throwing themselves on their knees in the thresholds of the neighboring houses, whose lips gave utterance to—

> "Where are you going, Jesus,
>   So gallant and so brave?"
>
> "I go," the Saviour smiling said,
>   "A contrite soul to save:
> For I must lead the penitent
>   Unto the promised land,
> Although they have more flagrant sins
>   Than the sea has grains of sand."

The tinkling of the passing bell announced, and two files of men, with long wax candles in their hands, preceded the priest, who bore with him that Lord for whose clemency no hut is too small, for whose grandeur no palace is sufficient. A military band, playing solemn music, followed a few paces in the rear.

"What music and what chanting is this I hear?" asked the Asistenta of Maria.

"Señora," she replied, "it is the music and chanting of those who by the direction of the marquis accompany His Majesty to your residence."

"What pomp! what ostentation! so much for me, and so little for God!" cried the señora.

Fernando and one of his cousins, carrying candles, then went out to meet the August Guest, and preceded Him to the chamber of the patient.

And now, propped up with pillows, the dying woman fixed her gaze on the image of her Redeemer, and received the *viaticum* with profound and tender adoration.

The ceremony being finished, she relapsed into a state of holy and tranquil meditation.

"Señora," said the confessor, after the lapse of a few minutes, "I know that all resentment against the marchioness has long since been extinguished in your breast."

"Oh, entirely, entirely! How much I grieve at not seeing her before I die!"

And scarce had she spoken, when the marchioness clasped her to her bosom, while Esperanza fell sobbing at the foot of the bed.

"Dear, dear sister, how much I thank you," sighed the Asistenta faintly as she fell back exhausted on her pillow. After a little while, she half opened her eyes and said, "Ines, my Elia, my poor child—alone—unprotected!"

The marchioness turned toward Elia, and, throwing her arms about her, exclaimed, "Sister, I accept the charge."

"My God," murmured the saintly woman, "I die tranquil—her fortune, her well-being, all is assured. May God bless you, my dear sister, and make life as sweet to you as you have made death to me!"

At the end of a minute, her confessor, leaning over her, heard proceed from her lips, with her latest breath, "Lord, receive my spirit."

"Thus," cried the priest aloud, "pass the souls of the just to the bosom of their God. Let us pray."

All prostrated themselves with the solemn

reverence caused by death, with the profound sentiment of piety it inspires, and the heart-rending grief it leaves behind in the breasts of those who survive their friends.

"My mother! oh, my mother!" cried the despairing Elia. They raised her in their arms, and, in spite of her resistance, carried her to her room.

"Leave, my daughter," said the marchioness, taking Esperanza by the arm, who with bitter sobs was kissing the hands of the corpse. "Go with Elia, and weep together as becomes two sisters who have lost their mother."

Esperanza hastened to obey.

The marchioness gave the necessary orders for preparing the body for interment, and was about to send for hired women for the purpose; but Maria would not hear of it. "No, señora," said she, "no mercenary hands shall touch my mistress. I alone will render her this last sad service."

They cleared the room, and then among the ample folds of the bed-curtains Don Benigno was observed, with eyes glazed and wandering, and fixed on the dead body of the señora; his hands were clasped and extended toward her, his lips without sound, his breast without sobs. They carried him away, and he suffered himself to be led along like a little child.

CHAPTER XXI.

On the following day, the cathedral bells uttered in mournful tones their solemn prayer for the dead—holy sounds which raise all hearts to heaven! Large wax candles, set in high candlesticks—like guards of honor for the dead—were placed on both sides of the staircase and corridors of the house of mourning. The drawing-room, in which were seated, in ceremonious order, the relatives and dear friends of the señora, was draped in black and lighted with tapers. In the adjoining room, Fernando, standing in the midst of a circle of his most intimate friends, received the compliments of condolence of those who with him had returned from attending the funeral service, celebrated with great magnificence in the parochial church; and this house, to which all Seville flocked, was nevertheless as empty as a head without a brain—a body without a soul—since she, whose presence there was like the spring, had that morning descended the grand staircase never to ascend it again, leaving a void in all hearts, an orphan in every poor man's home.

This sad ceremony continued nine days. On the tenth, Elia was in her room, which she had not left since the Asistenta's death.

By her side was the good Doña Marianita, who had always been fond of Elia, and now loved her more dearly than ever, out of respect to the memory of her aunt. She was endeavoring to console Elia with the platitudes common to the occasion.

"There is a saint more in heaven," she said.

"Yes," answered Elia, "and one less upon earth."

"How many troubles God has spared her, by taking her to Himself!"

"And how much happiness have I been deprived of!"

"It is necessary, my child, to conform ourselves to the afflictions which God sends us in this vale of tears."

"It is natural to grieve over them; if not, they would not be afflictions, nor the world a vale of tears."

"But Elia, why are we endowed with reason?"

"To make us more sensitive than the brutes."

"But, my child, when there is no remedy?"

"Ah! this is the very reason why my heart is breaking," exclaimed Elia, hiding her face in the sofa, wet with tears.

Marianita fell back upon her commonplace consolations, without force, without logic, without effect; and which, nevertheless, do a great deal of good, since they show the good-will of the would-be comforter; and for the wounds of the heart there is no balsam but affection, which, if it does not heal, at least alleviates.

The marchioness now came in, and, upon beholding Elia, said: "My child, how is it that you are not in mourning?"

The unhappy child had not thought of it.

"Put on a black dress at once, my darling," continued the marchioness, "and come with me."

The young girl obeyed without question or reply, and followed the marchioness to the drawing-room, where she found all the household assembled. A notary public was seated at a table in the middle of the room, holding in his hand a large yellow document sealed with three seals.

Seated in a corner, dressed in deep black, and with his head bent down and his hands crossed, was Don Benigno, a prey to the most profound grief and the most intense anxiety.

But when he saw Elia he extended his arms toward her. She threw herself into them, and their sobs were mingled together.

"Calm yourself, my child," said the marchioness, "and sit down by my side; for the occasion demands your undivided attention."

"Señores," said the notary when silence was enforced, "here is the last will and testament of Doña Maria Isabel Orrea de Calatrava,—whom may God exalt!—drawn up in due form of law, signed, sealed and delivered in the presence of competent witnesses."

Elia rose. "Why must I be present at this cruel scene," she asked, "where my mother's voice seems to speak to me through the boards of her coffin?"

"Because," replied the marchioness, "this will concerns you, and it is necessary that you should be present when it is opened."

"But, señora," said Elia, imploringly, "this is a family affair, and I am a stranger."

"Elia," answered the marchioness, with mild firmness, "your remaining here is a duty I impose upon you, in virtue of the authority vested in me by your mother; it is an homage to her memory. And if there be more tenderness in weeping, there is more merit in respecting and obeying the wishes of those whom God has called to Himself."

Elia seated herself again, and the notary read the will, which, after various legacies, declared Elia sole heiress.

"Gracious Maria!" exclaimed she, the pallor on her countenance giving place to a scarlet flush—"gracious Maria!"

"Does it surprise you, my love?" said the marchioness; "it surprises no one else."

"My God!" answered Elia, "this is the only grief my holy mother ever caused me. Her affection has made her do this injustice to her relations.—Señor," she added, approaching the notary, "draw up a paper at once for me to sign, expressing clearly and plainly that I renounce this property in favor of the legitimate heirs; for I long to rid myself of the burden which oppresses and shames me."

The marchioness called to her. "Elia," said she with severity, "if you should sign such a paper, it would be null and void, since I, the guardian appointed by your dying mother, expressly forbid it; but, apart from all this, tell me how you dare to break the will of your mother, whose dead body is scarcely cold?"

"But why should I keep it—what am I to do with all this property?" exclaimed Elia, with the utmost simplicity and sincerity.

"It is yours," answered the marchioness; "time and experience will teach you its use and management."

"But I do not want it! I do not want it!" insisted Elia. "I yield it, as is natural, to its legitimate owners."

"And do you believe, my poor child," said the marchioness, "that we would receive property not left us by its possessor? If you have thought so, your innocence must serve as an excuse for the offence you ignorantly commit."

Upon hearing these last words, which the marchioness pronounced with grave dignity, Elia remained silent.

"Could you believe us capable," said Fernando, in a sweet voice, " of taking advantage of your noble and generous self-sacrifice ? "

" But what power in the world," said Elia, after a moment's reflection, " can force me to consider as mine that which I do not regard as such ? "

"The will of the testator," answered the marchioness, "the solemn voice of the dead, which you would disregard by relinquishing the property, as we should if we received it."

" What shall I do ? what shall I do ? " cried Elia, when she found herself alone with Maria and Don Benigno.

" Give them," said the former, " if your tender conscience troubles you, the Orrea property, which does not amount to much ; and keep that which came from the Calatravas, which is immense, and as much yours as the hairs of your head."

"What shall I do, Don Benigno?" asked Elia, without attending to what Maria had said.

"Render unto God the things that are God's, and to Cæsar the thing's that are Cæsar's," he replied, without hesitation.

"And to John Smith the things that are John Smith's," growled Maria, sarcastically.

Elia clasped the hand of the sympathetic Don Benigno, who understood her.

And yet the Baroness of San Bruno said that evening at a reception: "Have you heard the news? The Asistenta, who was in her dotage, has left all her property to that hypocritical little foundling, who is more artful than a serpent, and who, with this end in view, set the two sisters-in-law at loggerheads a few months since, who up to that time had been so fondly united. A sad blow to the proud Ines, who expected to exchange her shell of a house for the elegant mansion of the Calatravas! upon the opening of the will, I understand, there was the deuce to pay; and they say that the improvised heiress is so well satisfied, and so perfectly happy, that she will not wear mourning. Ah! she is a cunning one, and

Carlos, too, knew very well what he was about. Now he will marry her, and be master of all that immense property, and the marchioness will have to put up with it. She is well punished for her ridiculous pride and vanity, and no one will be sorry for her, you may depend!"

Such is the world! and so we fulfil the divine precept, to "love our neighbors as ourselves."

CHAPTER XXII.

The just and pious judgment of the baroness was repeated, by an officer recently arrived from Seville, in a crowded *café* at Madrid.

He formed one of a happy circle of young men seated around a table, upon which smoked a large bowl of punch.

None of them had observed a young man, in deep mourning, who was seated at a table behind them, with his head resting on his hands, and only raised, from time to time, to give an impatient glance at the door, as if he were expecting some one.

But scarcely had the officer finished speaking, when the stranger stood before him and said, haughtily, "Cavalier, what you have just said is an infamous slander."

The surprise which this abrupt interruption caused was so great and general, that all were silent.

"Sir," replied the officer at length, "by what right do you assume to be a judge of my actions?"

"By the natural right which every man has to stand up in defence of truth and justice."

"It is Don Carlos de Orrea," whispered one of the officer's friends in his ear.

"In that case," said the officer, "I wish it to be well understood that I did not design to offend Don Carlos de Orrea, and I was not aware of his being present."

"I do not doubt it," rejoined Carlos, whose voice was tremulous with indignation; "I do not ask satisfaction for an offence against my person, but for an outrage upon truth. I demand that you retract this vile calumny, if you have forged it; and if not, that you give me the name of its author."

"I would most willingly retract what does not concern me in the slightest degree, as I only repeat from hearsay, if the contrary were proved to me," rejoined the officer; "but the word of command I do not recognize out of the service."

"Very well, then," said Carlos, "I shall

expect to convince you of the truth with my sword."

"I am at your service."

"At six o'clock, to-morrow morning, I will be outside of the gate of Recoletos."

"You will not have to wait for me."

Carlos bowed, and left the group, so merry but a little while before, in a general consternation.

"He is right and so am I," said the officer. "Plague take the facility which we all have of talking about people we don't know!" and then he added to himself: "I have got myself in a nice fix with the king, who hates duels and has a most excellent memory. My poor mother, too, is a widow, and I her only son.—But let us not anticipate," he said aloud, "evils we cannot remedy. Let us go to the theatre to see Maiquey."

Carlos, upon leaving the *café*, fell in with a friend, and taking his arm, said: "I awaited you here, according to our agreement, to inform you of a project I had formed of returning to Seville. But matters have changed, and I have now to ask a favor of you," and he proceeded to narrate what had transpired at the *café* to his friend, who was grieved to learn that the favor expected of him was to be Carlos's second in a duel.

Duels were then of rare occurrence in Spain; the reason of this being easily understood when we examine the causes which make them so frequent in other countries. These are, most commonly, *an ostentation of bravery, and a sensitiveness arising from vanity.*

Opposed to which in Spain, at that epoch, were an easy tolerance, and a politeness unknown elsewhere; for men's minds were not then exasperated and embittered by politics, as they are now, nor were they goaded to madness, under the name of progress, by a partisan press. Besides, public opinion was against duels; and he who had expected to gain a reputation for courage by sending a challenge, would only have obtained the name of a bully and a braggart. We do not speak of the holy and noble religious ideas which then exercised an influence over all things and all men, because to mix them up now with the affairs of the world, which makes a boast of disregarding them, would be to confound the solemn notes of the organ with the discordant and noisy sound of drums and trumpets.

Add to this, that the king was bitterly opposed to this remnant of barbarism, which, while it exists, will prevent the nineteenth century from boasting of having shaken off all the dust of the dark ages.

It is asserted by some, who are disposed to be nice upon points of honor, that duels are a perpetual check upon the insolent, and cannot be avoided; but we hold that they can be without laws, prohibitions, or punishments, by simply observing the noble quality of respect. Let us respect one another; because the upright and honorable have a right to claim respect and politeness as their due, and for those who are not so, they are the most difficult barriers to surmount. He who expects to conquer through insolence deceives himself, for, however he may excel in this most amiable accomplishment, he can hardly expect to pass through life without meeting an antagonist more insolent than himself.

Carlos went to his lodgings, wrote several

letters, and tore up various papers. Among these he found the only remembrance Elia had ever given him. It was a picture representing Cupid seated on the ground, holding in his hand a rose whose thorns had pierced him. Under it was written in a fine hand—

" The thorns for me, the roses for you."

Carlos kissed the keepsake a thousand tiems, and watered it with his tears, and then wrote a long and passionate letter to Elia, which he directed to her under cover to Fernando, to be delivered to him in case he should be killed. On the following morning, at half-past six o'clock, the officer lay upon the ground with a deep gash in his head, and Carlos, run through the body, was carried, in a senseless condition, to a mean-looking house in an out-of-the-way street of Madrid.

CHAPTER XXIII.

The marchioness had taken Elia to her house, where she was the object of the tenderest attentions from both mother and daughter. But Elia said nothing about her future prospects, which made the marchioness uneasy.

She thought at times that Elia might, as the mistress of so large a fortune, suppose that the objections to her marriage with Carlos would no longer exist. It was not impossible, too, that if Elia's stay in her house should be prolonged, Carlos might cherish vain hopes, and return unexpectedly to compromise her authority as a mother, and the hospitality she had so generously extended to the disconsolate orphan intrusted to her care. Delicacy forbade her taking the initiative in the question of Elia's plans for the future; but one day the subject came up naturally.

They were seated in a room looking out on the garden, and Elia was embroidering an altar-cloth on the same frame with Esperanza, when the marchioness said to her: "Elia, you have known Lorenzo Riosecco for some time, have you not?"

"Yes, señora," Elia answered; "I met him frequently at the house of my benefactress."

"He is the son," continued the marchioness, "of an excellent lady, a friend of mine, and of my deceased sister, and of a distinguished but poor family. He is a lieutenant-colonel in the army, and would be a colonel if he had money enough to purchase his commission. You know his fine manners and person, but you do not know, as I do, the nobility of his sentiments, the cultivation of his mind, and his exemplary deportment. He has loved you ever since he first saw you, and although his love is not necessary in a marriage where every thing is suitable and promises happiness to both parties, yet it is better that it should exist than not. He wishes to make you his wife, and I have promised his mother to urge his suit with all the influence I can command, because I believe he will make your happiness, as you will make his; and I feel it to be my duty to urge this marriage upon you, since, if you give him wealth, he will confer upon you position and distinguished rank in the world."

Elia did not raise her head while the marchioness was speaking. She turned deathly pale, and a feeling of humiliation, such as she had not experienced upon prostrating herself and kissing the hand of an infamous bandit, calling him *father*, now overcame her, causing her to cast her beautiful eyes in sadness to the ground.

But resisting this impulse of a superior soul which feels itself undervalued, she answered, sweetly but firmly, while large tears, pure and silent as her grief, ran down her cheeks:

"Señora, long before my dear mother died, my resolution was irrevocably fixed: my intentions were, and I have not altered them, to return to the convent after her death. I have come to your home solely for the purpose of demonstrating to you how grateful I feel for all your kindness; otherwise I should be with the nuns, now my sisters on the earth, as they will be hereafter in heaven."

The marchioness looked at Elia with admiration: now that she no longer feared her, she could appreciate the beauty of her character. She felt that it was sublime, at her age, with her beauty and wealth, to renounce a world that courted her, and a lover who adored her. This was an elevation of soul, a denial of self, which moved her profoundly. A tear stole to her eyes, as she fixed them upon that tender flower of the convent, and she felt an irresistible impulse to clasp her to her heart.

"My child," said she, after a short silence, "I admire your resolution, without approving it. Before taking so decisive a step, it is necessary to examine thoroughly your inclinations; and this is not done in one day, nor in two. At your age they are changeable. Your life is just beginning; do not decide lightly upon your future. Consider well the advantages of your position, which age and experience will make you appreciate more than you do now."

At this instant the Countess of Medina was announced, and the marchioness went out to receive her.

"Don't separate yourself from me," said

Esperanza, throwing her arms about Elia, "let us remain united, and marrying, as our mother desires, live tranquilly and happily."

Elia could only reply with her tears, as she withdrew precipitately to her room.

There she encountered Don Benigno, who had come to see her. He was talking to Maria, but they did not seem to agree. Maria was excited, Don Benigno as impenetrable as ever, but shaking his head, as a sign of disapproval of what Maria had just said.

Elia entered, drying her tears.

"Gracious!" exclaimed Maria, "what is the matter? What afflicts you, my darling? Have they said any thing to offend you, or hurt your feelings?"

"No, no," Elia answered quickly; "on the contrary, they have given me new proofs of interest and affection. I weep, Maria, upon parting with those who have been so kind to me in my deep affliction."

"That's another thing," answered Maria, "and I approve of your determination; but where do we go?—to Madrid I hope?"

"I am going into the convent," said Elia.

"To the convent!" echoed Maria; "have you lost your senses? What will the prince say when he comes to seek the shepherdess?"

"He will find her dead to the world, Maria, and the companion of angels. Princes do not marry shepherdesses except in your fables."

"But have you considered, blind one, that if the señora left you all her property, it was with the expectation that it would return with you to the family?"

"You deceive yourself, Maria," said Don Benigno; "our deceased lady—may she rest in peace!—had no other intention, in leaving her fortune to her adopted daughter, than to do her, in death as in life, all the good in her power."

"Don Benigno speaks the truth," said Elia, "his correct judgment is never at fault, passion does not blind, nor interest influence; nor is he to be diverted from the right path by the world's clamor. Your gray hairs, Maria, have not calmed the excitement of the brain they cover, while your excessive love for me clouds your reason. For me there are but two existences possible: the one brilliant but full of strife, the other humble but of unalterable tranquillity; the former at variance with my character, the latter adapted to it. I choose that which suits me. Our benefactress left you an independence. Remain, then, and take care of Don Benigno, in the house which she sanctified by her presence when living, and which must not be profaned by strangers now that she is no more."

"Don Benigno does not need my services," Maria answered quietly; "he can stay at home with Pedro. Do you suppose I am going to let you go into the convent without me?"

Elia threw herself into her arms.

She then closeted herself with Don Benigno, took the step she had long meditated, and made the following dispositions. At her death the property was to pass to the Orreas. In the mean time, the income (with the exception of a fifth, which was to go to the poor) would be appropriated to paying taxes, and improving and adding to the landed property. Don Benigno was appointed administrator.

Maria, upon witnessing "so many absurdities," did not deign to combat them. She retired, like Achilles, to his tent, thinking that the year of novitiate contained many days in which many thing might happen. She said to herself that, in supposing Carlos would remain quiet during this period, they were reckoning without their host, and she threw glances of anticipated triumph at Don Benigno, which did not seem to affect him in the least, nor make him depart, in the slightest degree, from his chronometer habits of life.

Some days after Elia had declared her intentions to the marchioness, the latter, finding her resolution inflexible, took her to the convent.

"I deliver to you," she said to the lady abbess, "this your daughter as pure as she was when she left the convent. It is meet that this angel should be the bride of Heaven; for she has chosen that better part which shall not be taken away from her."

Esperanza embraced Elia tenderly, and sobbed aloud.

Elia passed in through the iron door, which was closed behind her.

As the marchioness turned to depart, she met Maria and Don Benigno, in charge of Elia's baggage.

"And so, Maria, you are going to shut

yourself up in the convent with Elia? This is a proof of fidelity and attachment which does you honor."

"Yes, señora," answered Maria, "but I am going for the purpose of begging her day and night not to take the veil."

"And you have come too, Don Benigno?" said the marchioness, without answering Maria.

"Yes, señora; I come to congratulate her upon her holy choice."

"Go along with you, Señor Don Benigno, blessed of God!" said Maria, on taking leave of him. "You have been placing fuel on the altar for the sacrifice of this poor lamb. And you think you deserve the degree of doctor because you have helped with your wise sayings to separate two beings who were born for each other, which is against the law of Nature and of God. And this too from you, who pretended to love her so much! One lives to learn."

"Maria," answered Don Benigno, "you are blind as a mole."

"And do you pretend to be as far-seeing as an eagle?"

"If I do not see far, I see correctly."

"Correctly the length of your nose," remarked Maria.

"Come, Maria, after living together as friends for thirty years, let us part as such."

"Friends? No, sir! I am not a friend of any one who wishes ill to my child, and makes a compact with the *Queen of Egypt*, your servant, Don Benigno. Enemies! Yes, sir; enemies even to the valley of Jehoshaphat!"

So saying, she went with hasty steps into the convent.

CHAPTER XXIV.

CARLOS awoke from a state of insensibility which seemed to him a long dream. He sat up in bed, supporting himself on his elbow, and looked about the strange room. Suddenly he uttered a cry of joy that aroused the watcher by his bedside, whom want of rest had overpowered, and throwing his arms around his neck sighed in a feeble voice, "My brother! my dear brother!"

It was, in fact, Fernando, who, as soon as he heard of the duel, hastened to Madrid, to take care of Carlos, he being on this occasion, as on all others, his defender, his refuge, the noble type in fine of the firstborn who, with the consecrated right of primogeniture, unites the protection of a father with the sympathy of a brother.

After the first outburst of affection, Carlos asked anxiously how his mother had borne the news of his unfortunate affair; but Fernando tranquillized him by the assurance that it had been carefully concealed from her, and that she attributed his illness to natural causes.

To his eager inquiries about Elia, Fernando answered that she was at their mother's house, and tenderly cared for. These words caused in Carlos the wildest delight, and gave birth to the most flattering hopes.

But Fernando was too upright and sincere not to dispel them immediately. So he said to his brother:

"Don't flatter yourself, Carlos, nor take mother's noble and generous conduct as a proof that she desists from her reasonable opposition to your designs. Elia's great wealth, which in the eyes of the world would seem to approximate distances—these riches, which *raise* if they do not *exalt*, are, my brother, a new obstacle to your desire; for mother would consider herself debased if she gave to Elia rich the name of daughter which she denied to Elia poor; and she would regard you as having forfeited your rank in the world if you should owe your fortune to a woman separated from you by all the steps of the social ladder. It was difficult, but within the range of possibility, for her to raise from the gutter an unworthy daughter-in-law; but to seek her on a pile of gold—never, my brother, no, never! Could you believe, Carlos, that, under any circumstances, mother would tolerate seeing the cord of the hangman and the shackles of the galley-slave suspended from the proud branches of her genealogical tree— that she would consent to have the stain of illegitimacy upon her unsullied title-deeds? Carlos, you are still delirious with fever if you dream of such a thing! Would you, forsooth, exact from the marchioness of Val-de-Jara that which the humblest man of honor would not consent to? Besides, Elia has decided to return to the convent, her only home, as she calls it, and she is right; for it is the true home of innocence and virtue."

Carlos made a gesture of indignation as he exclaimed:

"Mother has persuaded her to this! She wishes to sacrifice this angel to her pride; but she will be disappointed! If there is merit in not opposing the will of a just and affectionate mother, there is weakness in submitting to a hard and-inflexible one, in whom pride smothers all generous feeling! And these are the people," he added, bitterly, "who call themselves religious and speak of Christian virtue; who wish to introduce religion into politics, and yet drive it from their own firesides!"

"Carlos!" said Fernando, severely.

"Is it, then," continued Carlos, vehemently, "is it Christian humility to break two hearts and destroy two existences only through pride? Is it a religious spirit that makes a prison of a convent? No; in hearts hardened by vile worldly interests true religion does not dwell!"

"If the state of physical suffering in which I find you," said Fernando, "did not awaken a softer emotion—that of pity in me—I should feel indignant at your language. It is a pretty piece of arrogance in you, truly, to set yourself up as a judge of the duties and virtues of others, and not to tolerate a person's being religious without being perfect, and perfect after your own manner of thinking. That a Christian loses all right to interfere in worldly affairs is a ridiculous absurdity! And is it, then, religious virtue in a mother to suffer her son to be carried away by his first amorous impulses, and contract a marriage that would embitter his life? Consider, Carlos whether or not mother would do right to let you marry a woman whom your friends—apostles of equality—would to-day approve and to-morrow be the first, perhaps, to treat with contempt; for the theories advanced to-day are to the experience of ages what paper money is to gold. What is really hard and unjust, from every point of view, is, the judgment that you have dared to form of your mother. And is it possible that the righteous will of an offended mother, which a Capuchin breaks like a reed, that tender reconciliation on the bed of death with a sister who had caused all her sorrow, and disinherited her children for a stranger; that protection so generously extended to one who, although innocently, has embittered her life, and threatened the honor of her house, that life which has been and is a model of austerity and virtue—is it possible, I say, that all this, which society remembers and admires, her own son neither sees nor appreciates, simply because she opposes what all the world condemns?

You say, my brother, that pride blinds; alas! how much greater blindness is produced by other passions!"

"Yes," answered Carlos, bitterly; "the generous protection offered and the manner of extending it, which consists in persuading a timid girl to immure herself in a convent, is a model of Jesuitical hypocrisy. But you admirably defend it all. For a second Ananias there could no doubt be readily found another Tertullus."

"And there is not wanting, to an unreasonable brother who reproaches, a reasonable one who forbears," said Fernando.

"Pardon, my brother," exclaimed Carlos; "my hot blood often makes me say what my heart has no part in."

"So I believe," answered Fernando, "but you deceive yourself in supposing that mother has persuaded Elia to the course she is taking; on the contrary, I can assure you, that she has begged her to defer the execution of her resolve. Mother is too upright and high-minded to resort to underhand measures to attain her object. She trusts simply in the justice of her cause, and the strength of her will. If at heart she cannot but approve of Elia's determination, it is because she feels that her position in the world, which flatters while it looks down upon her, which smiles yet wounds, is a false one, in which that innocent girl could never find happiness nor even contentment. Too humble to rise above the world's verdict, too timid to face it, and too delicate not to feel wounded by it, she has exactly the qualities which would hinder her from enjoying the advantages of her station, while she would be made to feel all its disadvantages."

"But do you suppose, Fernando," said Carlos, "that I can reconcile myself to her loss? You seem to forget me entirely. I will not consent to her sacrificing herself! What would remain to me in life without her?"

"Forgetfulness!" answered Fernando.

"Forgetfulness, Fernando! you insult me! Forgetfulness?"

"Yes, brother, yes! But I do not mean the forgetfulness which blots out the image of the past, but that which blunts its impressions. Our hearts refuse to recognize the word, even while they are yielding to its influence. God has made forgetfulness a moral necessity of our existence, as respiration is a physical one; and so our souls inhale it, as our lungs do the air, by an involuntary impulse."

"Your words are worthy of the cold son of a selfish mother!" exclaimed Carlos.

"Carlos," continued Fernando, "the fire of the passions is fed by tears and inflamed by lamentations. There is but one way to avoid its ravages, and that is by stifling it!"

"Impossible!" cried Carlos.

"You deceive yourself," answered Fernando, in a voice profoundly moved; "it is possible, and what I have affirmed by words I can prove by acts!"

Upon hearing the sad tone of Fernando's voice, Carlos turned his head and looked at him intently. His fine countenance was as pale as marble, and his eyes had that vague look known only to those who have suffered some great and hidden grief.

"Fernando! Fernando!" said Carlos, "I comprehend! From your childhood you have loved her! Yes, you love her!—you love Clara."

"Do not pronounce her name," answered Fernando, "except as a sister, if you do not wish to deprive my suffering of its purity. Let my secret serve you as a proof that all good is possible, and then let it return to its tomb—my heart!"

"You are a hero!" exclaimed Carlos.

"No," replied Fernando, "but I am an honorable man. Come," he added, observing the increased agitation of his brother, "this conversation has already been carried too far. It is necessary that you should keep quiet and calm yourself. The great thing is for you to reëstablish your health."

Pretty soon Carlos was enabled to leave his chamber. Then Fernando informed him that the mother of the officer, who, although recovering, had been at the point of death, was determined to prosecute him, and had succeeded in getting a number of affidavits showing him to have been the aggressor, and that the king was furious about the whole matter.

There remained, then, to Carlos only the alternative of exile or imprisonment; he could not reasonably refuse to adopt the former, the more especially as he felt sure that if he were once in prison, his mother would take care that he was not released from it until Elia had taken the veil. He set out, then, with tears of sorrow and anger, trusting in the promise his brother made him, to do all in his power to obtain his pardon from the king. He left a letter for Elia, in which he told her that he would be absent two months on public service, and that he was not opposed to her going to the convent, where she could tranquilly await his return. The whole letter was filled with the most passionate expressions of love and devotion, and he begged her a thousand times not to forget the promises she had made him, which gave him the right to claim her as his wife even at the foot of the altar.

Some days afterward, this letter reached the convent, that *receptacle of cold, egotistical souls*, according to the philosopher Narciso, and Carlos arrived in England, the *swan's nest*, as Shakespeare calls it; appellations which, in our opinion, might very properly be exchanged, and we see by your smile, gentle reader, that you agree with us.

CHAPTER XXV.

The marchioness was not ignorant of Carlos's duel, although she appeared so. It caused her profound affliction; nevertheless, she answered the friend who told her of it: "If all men acted as he has upon hearing his mother slandered, evil-speakers would put a rein upon their tongues."

But while Fernando was urgently soliciting his brother's pardon at Madrid, his mother contrived, through her friends and relations, to have it delayed; for she was anxious that Carlos should not return until Elia had professed; for the simple reason that she desired to avoid a scene, so exceedingly repugnant to one of her grave and quiet character. So Fernando could only console his brother with the hopes that the prime minister held out to him, at each succeeding interview. These delays exasperated Carlos, who, with his Spanish constancy to his lady-love and native country, cursed his banishment. All the splendor of London passed before his eyes unheeded, without interesting his mind or his heart. At the parties of the nobility, where he felt as much bored as an old millionnaire lord, he scarcely deigned to notice the ardent and languid glances of the Englishwomen, who, in imitating the maidens of Italy, have surpassed them in coquetry.

He became very sad under that ash-colored sky, which seems to be the first attacked by the national disease, *spleen*—in that foggy atmosphere, which envelopes the great city like a shroud, and is overhead a night without stars and without repose. The trees, stripped of their leaves, seemed black, from their contrast with the snow-drifts, which covered the earth, and raised their long arms to heaven, like skeletons asking for burial.

To Carlos the days seemed endless, and the nights eternal; and yet the months were swiftly revolving round the dial-plate of Time. And soon the dying groans of Winter were heard in the equinoctial storm, and Spring commenced her flowery reign. The fields put on their brightest smiles, and decked themselves in garments of various colors, and life seemed a sylvan poem. But nothing spoke to the heart of the exile, filled with recollections of the past and hopes for the future.

His situation became intolerable when he reflected that in two months Elia would have finished her novitiate. He awaited, however, the arrival of the latest period designated by Fernando for the reception of his pardon; but when this came and he found that it was only another link in the chain, forged to keep him absent, he became indignant, and resolved to return to Spain, let what would be the consequence. How his heart beat with joy when he descried Spain looming up on the horizon! The pure blue of heaven and the brilliant blue of the sea seemed to be parted, like a turquoise-shell, for the sole purpose of showing in their embrace beautiful Cadiz, the white pearl of the Atlantic! He saw on his left hand the city of San Lucar, at the mouth of the silvery Guadalquivir, and ahead and on his right Rota, Santa Maria, Puerto Real, the island of San Fernando, and Medina, a city on a rock, resembling a nest of alabaster. He beheld in the bay that moving forest of masts, browned by the suns of the tropics, hardened by the snows of the poles, displaying the names of their countries from their mast-heads, in their language of many colors, and resting with furled sails, like birds who have folded their wings, trusting to their anchors, fit emblems of hope. He fixed a grateful glance upon the lighthouse of San Sebastian, which Cadiz has built on a reef, in the midst of the sea, in order that the noise of the city may not distract it, while that of the waves reminds it of its holy mission—Cyclops of granite, sleepless mariner, eternal "lookout," whose feet are washed by the sea, whose forehead is wet with foam; Christian vestal, watching this small flame which gives so much light! holy flame whereby charity displays, amid the treacherous darkness, the word "Beware!" finger of fire which indicates the danger night hides; wise counsellor who through darkness and tempest, amid the waste of waters, points out the course to steer, and unites in bonds of sympathy those who wander, beset by danger, with those who rest secure; temple of charity which the angels point out to God, in proof of man's remembrance of the teaching of the Apostle Paul!

Over this enchanting picture was the sky of Andalusia, decked in smiles—that sky always serene, always peaceful—which never covers itself with clouds except when the parched earth cries, "I am thirsty. Give me drink."

Carlos had no sooner arrived in Cadiz, than he embarked for Santa Maria in a felucca that attracted him with its half-arrogant, half-pious inscription on the stern:

> "With God I sail,
> With good deeds court the gale!"

Unfurling her enormous lateen sail, which expanded to the breeze as the heart of a wanderer expands upon beholding his native land, the felucca darted through the waves, which broke in soft ripples against her sides. The bar at the mouth of the Guadalete being passed, the master of the little craft took off his hat, and repeated in a loud voice a *Pater noster* for the souls of the many who have been wrecked on that dangerous shoal! a holy offering to the dead which those should respect, from motives of humanity, who do not reverence it from devotion; and yet this pious custom has been abolished, through the sarcasms of the world. So have the impious added to the enlightenment of the nineteenth century by suppressing this prayer in the mouth of the common people.

Carlos reached Santa Maria, after a few hours' sail, and then drove twelve miles in a light carriage, to San Lucar, where he took a steamboat for Seville, the bride of the Guadalquivir, whose loves were known to the ancient poets as they are known and celebrated by the modern; for love has no secrets from poetry, nor poetry from love, as there are none between body and soul. He arrived at night. The moon threw a soft light over the silent city, lulled to rest by the song of the nightingale, which produces an indescribable emotion in the heart and fills the eyes with tears. The notes of a solitary guitar fell upon his ear, and, moved by the breeze, the orange-trees refreshed him with their sweet-smelling fans.

Carlos strolled about the *paseo de las delicias* until a late hour, and then betook himself to an inn, in an obscure street, where he passed the night.

CHAPTER XXVI.

On the following morning, just as the cathedral clock was striking seven, a young man knocked at the door of the nunnery of *Madre de Dios*.

"I will call the door-keeper," said a well-known voice.

"Maria!" cried Carlos.

"Who calls me by name?" asked the voice.

"Don't you know me, Maria?"

An exclamation of joy was the response, and rapid steps were heard moving away.

"I knew it," cried Maria, "I knew he would come. I have never doubted him for an instant, for I know what love is!"

The door-keeper soon came, and, finding that Carlos was the son of the Marchioness of Val-de-Jara, showed him to the visitors' parlor.

This was a long, narrow room, with a strong iron grating at one end of it, behind which a black curtain was closely drawn.

Over the grating was the following inscription:

"*Nostra conversatio in cœlis est.*"

On the opposite side, a small, grated window, near the ceiling, admitted a pallid, mournful light, which faded entirely away upon the black curtain. On the wall, opposite to the door of entrance, hung an immense picture representing Saint Cecilia, renouncing at her marriage the seductions of love, converting her husband to the spiritualism of her own exalted faith, and transforming the marriage-bed into an altar, crowned by the angels with white roses.

A number of high-backed wooden chairs were placed against the cold, white walls, and a pine table, painted black, stood in the middle of the floor.

Carlos felt, upon entering this gloomy room, as if a cold hand had been placed upon his heart, and had stopped its beating. Thus it happens to the brilliant bird of the tropics, whose destiny takes it to the stunted pines of

Lapland. It shivers with cold, its wings droop, and its song dies in its throat.

Carlos sank into a chair. Suddenly the curtain was rapidly drawn. A large, well-lighted apartment appeared to his bewildered eyes, and standing in the middle of it was Elia.

"Oh, Carlos!" she exclaimed in an accent expressive of the most perfect affection, "what pleasure it gives me to see you here on this happy and solemn day, when I am about to pronounce my vows! Only you, among all those whom I love and who love me, were wanting!"

Carlos fixed his eyes upon Elia, as upon an enigma he could not understand.

Nothing could have been more beautiful than that enchanting apparition, surrounded by a halo of light. Her eyes shone with heavenly brilliancy, the reflection of her pure and loving soul. A handkerchief thrown over her head, and drawn closely under the chin, served to display the perfect oval of her face. Her white habit, falling in broad folds to the ground; the veil, which waved from her head to her feet, gave to that youthful figure a grave and soft dignity which filled the beholder with awe as well as admiration. At that instant it seemed to Carlos that his hopes withered like flowers plucked from the earth and placed on the altar of a saint. But stifling this feeling— "I come not, Elia," said he, "to witness your vows; I come to prevent your taking them. I come to fulfil my promise, and to exact the fulfilment of yours. Can you have forgotten them? Is the past blotted from your memory?"

"All has been blotted from my heart, in the convent, except gratitude, which fills it all."

"And dare you say this?" exclaimed Carlos. "Dare you, with this same hand which dispenses alms, dries the tears of those who suffer and decks the altars with flowers, drive a dagger into the heart of the man who loves you! the companion of your childhood—of him whom your mother called son?"

"I dare," answered Elia, "withdraw myself from him in order to turn him aside from the path of error, and guide him to that which it is his duty to follow."

"These are the ideas instilled into you in

the convent! Oh, Elia! the path you have marked out will lead you to sacrifice and me to desperation! Will you destroy the felicity of the man who adores you? You so good, so amiable—can you be ungrateful and cruel? So young, so beautiful! will you be so insensate as to renounce the joys of life and obstinately adhere to a resolution all must condemn?"

"And who can blame me," answered Elia, "for desiring to separate myself from a world which each one of its inhabitants execrates? Find me a single one who is content with his lot; find me but one who can say: 'The world has given me true happiness, an unalterable tranquillity: I have preserved in it a pure conscience, a heart free from animosity; no word, no look has ever wounded me. I have lived without fears and without hopes, or I have seen the former realized and the latter vanish without anguish or depression of spirits. I have seen youth pass away without regret, and old age arrive without repugnance!' Show me but one, Carlos, who can say this, and it will be a practical eulogium of the world—a sound argument that will convince me. The glance I cast upon society was brief but lucid, and has produced its effects upon my heart. My reason, if the finger of God were wanting, would have led me in the sweet path I am following, and I will not wander from it. Yes, Carlos, my days of silence and prayer will glide away peacefully and happily, and be as sweet as the drops distilled from the honey-comb."

"Elia," answered Carlos, "you are under the influence of a religious excitement which obscures your vision, like a cloud of incense, blinding you with regard to the future. You know not your own heart, and are deceiving yourself as to its aspirations. But I will never consent," he added, with intense agitation, "to your burying yourself in the convent. You have plighted your troth to me; you have sworn to be mine. I have a right to claim you as my wife, and I shall find means to enforce this right!"

"Your right!" exclaimed Elia in a tone of reproof. "Where is it? What is it? Am I what I was? Are there not between us the world and a mother's prohibition? Dare you come to snatch me from the foot of the altar—dare you say to me, 'I deprive you of a peaceful and happy life, and I offer you in exchange the ephemeral felicity of earthly love?' Dare you tear me from the Church, as a maniac would drag a child from its mother's bosom? No, no! abandon all hope. We are as widely separated as the sun that surrounds itself with light and noise, and the moon that seeks silence and the night. Follow the rapid and impetuous current of your destiny, and do not attempt to carry with it the feeble flower you have found on its margin, and which would only perish by the union. So, Carlos, you are the blind one, blinded by passion; for this truly blinds, and not the incense of which you have spoken, which only serves to direct our eyes toward the heaven to which it ascends."

"Elia, why do you talk thus?"

"Because, Carlos, it is blind passion that urges men to set public opinion at defiance, and overturn an established order; and this cannot guide, but needs to be guided."

"How tranquil, how serene, how composed you are!" said Carlos, angrily.

"Because I have prayed, Carlos."

"You have never loved me, Elia!" exclaimed Carlos, falling into a chair, and covering his face with his hands.

"Oh, yes! I have loved you, and still love you, Carlos," answered Elia, in a soft and sweet voice. "But in this infinite love that I bear you there is neither presence nor absence; nor past, present, nor future; time glides over it as over eternity, without changing or disturbing it. It is a love which does not distract the heart from God, but is identified with God, the fountain and end of all love! It is a love that does not fear ingratitude, because it exacts nothing in return; it is an unchangeable love, that is heard in prayer, and ascends with it to heaven. It is a love like that of the stars, and must be confined to its proper sphere. We may go to them hereafter, but they will not come to us here."

"But this love," said Carlos, sorrowfully, "this love which separates those who feel it upon earth, does not bring happiness, Elia."

"What do you call happiness?" asked Elia. "If it is the peace which repose of conscience and freedom from the sway of the passions bring; if it is the soft calm which is felt when the past is without remorse and the future without fears; if it is found in a life whose dreams are peaceful whose waking hours are calm and cheerful; if it consists in awaiting death without desiring or fearing it, if this be true happiness and without alloy—why, then I have comprehended it, Carlos, and have made it mine."

Carlos, keeping his face still covered, rested his head on the back of his chair; tears trickled through his fingers, and his whole frame shook with his convulsive sobs.

"Carlos, Carlos!" continued the distressed Elia, in a tone of supplication. "Do not afflict me with your tears; do not disturb my heart with your sorrow. Love me ever, but do not strive against Heaven. Come, generously, and with religious feeling, to unite yourself to me on that height from which I contemplate the passions and interests of the earth; that height, Carlos—as I plainly saw in the world—is not attained by talent and genius, but by faith, that divine faith which fills the sea, and yet finds a lodging in the humblest heart. Don Narciso could not comprehend it, and yet it was plain and intelligible to Don Benigno. From this height, Carlos, life appears so short, so insignificant—the zero of eternity! and yet it can hold many tears and prepare fearful remorse for the future. Only on this height, Carlos, is one divested of ignominy inherited from one's forefathers, as are the sons of Adam of the curse he entailed upon them. There we lay aside our earthly bodies and soar toward heaven, as the loathsome caterpillar is changed to the butterfly. On this height, my brother, we are farther from the earth but nearer heaven, heaven," she repeated, raising her eyes and hands toward it, with holy exultation, " there, where all loving hearts will be united in that celestial and perfect love, which is beatitude! "

Elia, filled with the inspiration of the Holy Spirit, her face bathed in tears, appeared to Carlos a seraph, descended from heaven, and about to ascend to it again.

Moved, fascinated, swayed by a magnetic impulse, he knelt down; and resting his bowed head against the bars of the grating—

"I find at last—unfortunately for my happiness too late," he exclaimed, "that in the midst of the base materialism of the world, there are beings whose souls shine like divine torches in the darkness, like beacon-lights at night, who are so exalted that passion profanes them, and who should only be loved upon the earth as the angels are loved in heaven!"

EPILOGUE.

If you should ask me what became of those who remained amid the great and shifting scenery of the world,—it being the duty of the novelist to give an account of the personages whom he places on the stage,—I might answer as Schiller replied to those who questioned him concerning Theckla:

"Do you ask the trees of winter, perchance, what has become of the nightingales whose songs charmed you in the spring? They lived only while they loved."

Nevertheless, life is divided into two parts; the ideal and the material; and we will speak of the second, which outlives the first.

Fernando died at Madrid, in the unfortunate affair of the 7th of July, 1822, defending the king.

Carlos, faithful to a cause already lost, fell

at Trocadero in the following year, in that disastrous battle where blood was shed without enthusiasm, men fought without hope, and death was met bravely, but to no purpose.

The marchioness bore with fortitude the loss of Fernando, that beloved and perfect son, who had realized her fondest expectations; but the death of Carlos destroyed her. He was the last of the Orreas, and the first who had died defending a cause which was not that of his king, his country, and his religion. Her haughty spirit gave way, and she died in the arms of the inconsolable Esperanza.

This perfect daughter married a distinguished and worthy man, and had two sons. The elder, brought up at home under the eyes of his parents, joined the ranks of Don Carlos, and was slain at the siege of Bilbao; the younger, educated in the artillery-school at Madrid, made his first campaign under General Cordoba, the commander-in-chief of the queen's forces, and met death in the battle of Mendigorria.

When Esperanza, wild with grief at seeing these idols of her heart fall victims to that terrible civil war—the most frightful scourge that man has ever framed with his own hands—felt her reason giving way, she went to the convent to see Elia—and returned from it, calm and resigned.

END OF ELIA.

CONSOLATION IN DEATH.

CONSOLATION IN DEATH;

OR,

A MOTHER'S PRAYER TO THE VIRGIN.

CHAPTER I.

In the spacious bay of Cadiz, between the port of Santa Maria and the city of San Fernando, stands Puerto Real, the most modest and unassuming of the neighbors of Cadiz, notwithstanding the nobility of its origin, it having been founded, as its arms and beautiful name attest, by the Catholic Sovereigns.

This town is the resort of the wealthy merchants of Cadiz, who have erected here houses and churches which would not bring discredit on the capital itself. It is chiefly noted, however, for the number and beauty of its gardens, filled with the rarest and loveliest flowers, in which the women of Cadiz seem to take as much delight as if they were daughters of Flora, instead of being the spoilt children of the Swan of the Ocean.

Puerto Real is separated from the bay by extensive marshes, covered with reeds, which the sea fills and empties, by turns, with its unceasing undulations. In the midst of these the industry of man has created the vast salt-works, so famous for the excellence and abundance of the salt which they produce. The view presented by these salt marshes is sad and monotonous in the extreme.

To the right of Puerto Real, on a projecting point of land, like Puntales on the opposite shore, is the famous Trocadero: the two forts, by common consent, seemingly having drawn near to each other, for the purpose of keeping watch and ward, like two valiant sentinels, over one of the three arsenals of the Peninsula. Trocadero on its side shelters Puerto Real from the fierce attacks of the ocean, which even the massive walls of Cadiz are unable to resist, so that, guarded by the fort and intrenched behind its marshes, the beautiful town sleeps peacefully amidst its flowers under the guardianship of its celestial patron, St. Roque. But although not in contact with the ocean, it does not the less enjoy a view of its grandeur and loveliness; and he who of an afternoon pensively reclines in the shade of the almond-trees whose branches overhang every path of its far-famed *paseo*, may see, on the right, a lovely country stretching far away to the highlands of Ronda; in front, the port of Santa Maria, ever gazing on its image in the placid waters of the Guadalete; and, on the left, Cadiz, with its rocks for a foundation, its walls for a pedestal, its towers a crown, its light-house a torch, and upon its snowy bosom, the church of Carmen—thrice holy scapulary, the pride of Andalusia; and finally he may behold, between Cadiz and Santa Maria, the immensity of the sea, and the monarch of day slowly descending beneath the waves, leaving, while he rests, his mission of light in heaven, to the stars, and on earth to the light-house, the holiest of all the monuments which man has erected upon the earth—after the temple of God!

CHAPTER II.

This beautiful view of the sea and the setting sun gave no pleasure, however, to a man who, on a bright afternoon in May, journeyed on his mule by the Quarry road, toward the town. Although but fifty years old his hair was of a silvery white, while the wrinkles which furrowed his forehead bore witness that sorrow had got the better of age in the sad mission of destroying the man. This person was an inhabitant of the town, named Antonio Parra, and married to one of those women who reconcile God with humanity; in whom all is heart, all compassion; who put in practice the divine teaching, *Love never wearies of doing good*, applying this not only to the love of family and neighbors but to one's bitterest and most implacable enemies. Love sublime! which descended from the Cross, but has become so corrupted, by its long residence upon earth, that when the generality of mankind behold it exhibited in some favored being, they either refuse to recognize it, or coldly deride it as hypocrisy.

One would have supposed that the marriage of this excellent couple must bring with it perfect happiness to both; but alas! happiness on earth is not the lot of man, who, through sin, degraded his own primitive being and that of his race. Toil for men, sorrow for women! who will remove this curse of God, which bows humanity to the ground?

Antonio and his wife, then, had been called to mourn, in succession, the death of two sons, killed in battle, and a daughter, snatched from them, in the bloom of youth, by that fatal malady which came from the Ganges to seek its victims. There remained to them now only the youngest child, Bernardo, who was commonly spoken of, in the neighborhood, as the Judas of the family. This boy, who, at the time of which I speak, was but twelve years of age, had all the bad qualities which spring the one from the other. Laziness had produced idleness, and this evil inclinations, which, unfortunately, the excessive love of his parents had prevented their correcting, or perhaps observing, until they had become so engrafted on his nature as to threaten his utter destruction body and soul.

✓ Whilst Antonio on his mule was slowly approaching home, his wife Maria was seated in the parlor of her house, with her little niece by her side, whom she was teaching to sew, and at the same time instructing in the Catholic faith.

"Veronica, my child," said the good woman, "do you think you know by heart now the story which your neighbor, the sacristan's wife, taught you?"

"Yes, aunt," replied the child, without ceasing to work on her samples, which seemed to afford her much pleasure, "and I will repeat it to you.

'In the midst of great Jerusalem,
  The city of the Jew,
An afflicted mother moved in haste,
  All clad in white and blue,
"Have you seen, perchance, good gentleman,
  My Son, my darling Son?"
"I saw Him pass this very spot,
  Just as the cock crowed one,

With a cross upon His shoulders,
   That caused him fearful pain,
And a crown of thorns upon His head,
   Whose nettles pierced His brain;
With the weight of His harsh burden,
   Three times the Saviour slips,
And thrice upon the rugged earth
   He pressed His sainted lips!
And then came out Veronica,
   A maid of humble race,
Who thrice knelt down upon the ground,
   And kissed the sacred place;
And then with snowy handkerchief,
   Of blood and dirt the trace
Removed from off that beauteous brow,
   Whereon rests Heaven's grace—
Three folds are in that handkerchief,
   Each bears the Saviour's face!"

*   *   *   *   *

One likeness is in Jaen found,
   The second is in Rome,
The third was thrown into the sea,
   To bless the sailor's home.'"

"Aunt," asked the child, as she finished her narration, "of what wood was that cross made, that it caused the Saviour to fall three times? What made it so heavy?"

"It weighed so much on account of its great size. The trunk was of cypress, its arms of palm, and the part on which Our Blessed Lord's feet rested of cedar, while the piece which was set up over His divine head bearing this inscription, '*This is Jesus, the King of the Jews,*' was of olive; all of which incloses a great mystery, my darling," answered the aunt. "But now," she continued, "you may leave your task, and go out to play."

The child folded her sampler with much neatness, taking care to put away her needle and thimble in a pocket which was attached to it, and then kneeling before an image of Our Lady which was placed upon a table, crossed her little hands, and said:

"'Mary Most Holy!
Thy servant doth pray
Thy divine license
To run out and play.
With thy blessed hand—
All grief redressing—
Virgin Immaculate,
Give me thy blessing!'"

Afterward she dressed a little clay doll, and

then, taking it in her arms, began to move to and fro, and sing to it the following:

> "'Every little doll
> Gives pleasure to me,
> Even clay ones that cost
> Of farthings but three.'

"Won't you go to sleep?" she added, seating her doll in her lap; "well, then, I will teach you to pray. In the morning the very first thing you should say is:

> 'Now blessed be the light of day,
> Which God bestows on all;
> Oh, bless Him for it, while you may,
> All things both great and small!'

And at night, this:

> 'With my Lord I go to rest,
> To sleep until the morn;
> No other better can be found,
> Nor was, nor will be, born.—
> If I sleep, dear Christ, awake me,
> And, if I die, oh, take me!'"

"Where can Bernardo have gone?" said the good mother at length. "It is near vespers; his father will soon be here, and if he does not find him at home, will be uneasy about him."

"He is playing bull-fight with the other boys," replied the child. "I cannot see what pleasure the boys find in such racing and shouting."

"What pleases boys cannot and should not please girls," responded her aunt, quickly, who always, instinctively, excused her son. "He will soon become more sedate, my child. We must have patience with him."

At this moment Bernardo dashed into the room, with his clothes all torn, and crying out at the top of his voice: "Hurrah for the bull! hurrah for the bull!"

"How in the world have you managed to tear your clothes so, my son?" asked his mother.

"How should I tear them but with a nail or some confounded hook?" answered the boy. "If you do not wish to see me in tatters, you should not make my clothes out of this miserable cloth!"

"Miserable cloth, my son? why, they are bran new, and made of the *bread of the poor*."

"Well, make them of the *bread of the rich*, then," replied the lad, disrespectfully. "Veronica," he continued, turning toward the child, "I saw your cat upon the roof of the house, and threw a stone at it. I hit it, but unfortunately did not kill it. I will do better next time."

"And what has my poor little cat done, that you should wish to kill it?" exclaimed Veronica, bursting into tears.

"Oh, what a goose to weep for a cat!" sneered the boy. "I have a good mind to dry your tears, Madame *Cry-baby*, with a handful of nettles."

"You are capable of doing any thing, Herod," replied the little girl, flying to her aunt for protection.

And now came the ringing of a bell, and then of another and another, as if the holy voice of the Church were many times repeating the words, "Pray, sinner, pray; for the day is ended, during which you have not died, and the night cometh, when your soul may be required of you."

The aunt and her niece, who understood perfectly this Catholic language, rose up at once, and the former said: "Come, Bernardo, salute the Virgin, and pray—this morning, remember, you were not willing to do so."

"Nor am I willing now," he replied, taking a handful of chestnuts out of his pocket and beginning to eat them.

His good mother, who knew by experience that she could effect nothing by reasoning with him, said, fetching a deep sigh, "Well, then, I will pray twice—once for you, and once for myself;" and, accordingly, she commenced the salutation to the Virgin, Veronica responding with her infantile voice, and both concluding their devotion in this manner:

> "Receive, Holy Mother,
>   Ave Marias three,
> Which thy sinful servant
>   Humbly offers thee.
> The first for those in agony;
>   For those in mortal sin
> The next—and wanderers of the sea
>   Must claim the third, I ween.
> Let not their hearts be hardened,
>   From grace ne'er let them fall—
> Oh, grant their sins be pardoned,
>   And Christ be with them all!"

> "And let these nuts be roasted,
>   Although so very small!"

—added Bernardo.

"Be silent, Bernardo!" said his afflicted mother. "What you say is irreverent."

At this instant the father entered.

"You do not know," he exclaimed, addressing his wife, "what this bad, this unfeeling boy has done."

The poor mother began to tremble, and, before ascertaining the cause for her grief, her eyes were filled with the tears which were destroying them.

"With a stone he has laid open the head of Juan de Silva," continued her husband.

"He threw at me first," said Bernardo pertly. "Who owes a debt and pays it, is an honest fellow!"

"It is false," replied the father; "a man who witnessed the occurrence told me all about it; but if the devil had not invented lying, you would have done so. Juan did not even see you when the stone struck him. A more provoking boy than you cannot be found in the town. And you are as bold about it as if you had done something meritorious. You neither feel regret for the sin you have committed, nor shame at being detected in a falsehood!"

"I have not told a falsehood," answered Bernardo. "Juan threw at me the other day, and I have been on the watch for him ever since."

"Oh, perverse child!" groaned the father. "At so early an age to bear malice! Who would suppose that this blessed woman brought you into the world, and that in your veins flows the honored blood of the Parras?"

"Who injures me has to pay for it," murmured the incorrigible boy, between his teeth.

The father sank into a chair, and indignantly threw his hat upon another.

"Don't you know, son," exclaimed Maria, "that the law of God commands us not to return evil for evil, neither by word nor deed, and that St. John says that he who hates his brother is a murderer?"

"Maria," said her husband, "I have told you before that this unnatural son is carrying me to my grave; while you are losing your eyesight from incessant crying. Depend upon it, he will come to a bad end."

"Holy mother! Virgin of mercy! grant that he become a Christian!" sobbed the sainted mother.

CHAPTER III.

TEN years afterward, and the prophecies of the old man were partly fulfilled.

Bernardo had continued in his evil ways, and on various occasions had come near meeting a disastrous end. His mother was almost blind from weeping, and the poor old father lay stretched upon the bed from which he was destined never more to rise.

"And has Bernardo not come in to-night either?" asked the sick man of his wife, who shook her head sorrowfully, but made no reply in words.

"Maria," continued her husband, "I am covered with shame through the acts of my own flesh and blood, and shame is a weighty cross which I cannot bear up under. My heart has been many years dead, and now my body is dying. This wicked son is burying me."

"Husband," replied his wife, concealing the tears which were choking her, "the lion is not so fierce as he is painted. Be hopeful; Bernardo will yet be a good son. The greater a sinner's faults are, the greater must be our patience with him."

"It is because we have been too patient and forbearing with him, Maria, that he is what he is If there were no receivers, there would be no thieves. We have always concealed his vices, and given him money to squander, and so it is that a part of his perdition falls upon us."

"What money could we give him, my husband, when our purse is in such a state that the rats may run through it?"

"He has reduced us to this impoverished condition, as you know, Maria, and there are not wanting persons who accuse him of being concerned in the robbery of a few nights since; and although it has not been proved against him, he has fallen into disrepute, and if *he* has the impudence to disregard these things, *I* have not, who have always been in the habit, heretofore, of wearing my hat thrown back and not down over my face."

"You well know that our poor son had nothing to do with the robbery, since that night he slept at home. Thus you see, my husband, how false appearances are."

"He slept at home, it is true," answered her husband, "thanks to a debauch; for out of the four-and-twenty hours, he passes five-and-twenty drinking. I am worn out, and glad to die, for sorrow has so consumed my flesh that there will be little left for the worms; but I grieve to leave you with no protection except the good God, to be tormented ever by this hard-hearted son, who, as I have often predicted, will come to a bad end."

"Mother of mercy," prayed the sobbing Maria, "*grant that he become a Christian!*"

Shortly after this scene the honored Antonio Parra expired in the arms of his afflicted companion, with all the divine consolations which make death holy, and all the human sympathy which makes it sweet; but without the presence of Bernardo, who was off on one of his usual frolics.

Veronica during this sad period was ever by the side of her aunt, endeavoring to lighten her labors, and after her uncle's decease she remained with her, like a good daughter, to comfort her in her loneliness.

She was now a pretty girl, very modest and retiring, and exceedingly religious. She dressed with great simplicity, and in excellent taste, and was beloved by the whole neighborhood for her sweet temper and obliging, amiable disposition.

On Bernardo the death of his father had produced but little effect, or at least had not had the effect of reforming his habits. It had rather served to break the last tie which bound him to virtue; for the respect with which his father's gray hairs (every one of which told of some sorrow caused by the son) had inspired him had restrained him from vice in the old man's presence. Shame had made him bow his head before him; for, though dissipated and vicious, he could not forget the words he had been taught to repeat upon his mother's lap—"*Love God above all things; honor thy father and thy mother.*"

And so, at first, he admired and almost envied his cousin for the manner in which she behaved toward his mother, after his father's death; and afterward, as he beheld her always true to herself, always amiable, always calm, she began to have for his restless spirit the soft attraction which a placid and tranquil haven has for the mariner who on the high seas struggles against the currents which are drifting him, and the hurricane which impels him onward.

But the ardent glances which Bernardo fixed upon his cousin prevented the modest and innocent girl from ever looking toward him even, and in fact his rough and sarcastic language had given her such a dislike to him that she avoided, as much as possible, being in his society, and selected the times when she knew he was absent for remaining with and comforting her aunt. This was not unnoticed by Bernardo; but he was one of those men whom an obstacle urges forward rather than drives backward; one of those blind worshippers of their own will who are wholly given up to obstinacy, that stupid mixture of ignorance and pride—the vice of children, the vice of fools, the vice, in short, of all those who delight in boasting of their own acts and in depreciating the acts of others!

As Bernardo did not think it possible that a woman could fail to love him, unless she loved another, he set himself to watch his cousin at all hours; but he could not discover any thing hidden in that existence which was gliding away, piously and silently, at the foot of the altar, and in the performance of good works at home and abroad; so he said to himself, "Either Veronica is not in love, in which case she will fall in love with me when I say to her, 'I adore you,' or else she is in love, and will not return my affection, in which event I shall know that her lover is Juan de Silva, who lives next door to her, and can converse with her without being observed." And being determined to know the truth, he awaited his cousin one evening, hiding behind a corner, so that when she turned it she met him face to face.

"I was waiting for you, Veronica."

"And what for?" she replied, instinctively alarmed.

"To tell you that I love you."

The effect of this abrupt declaration upon Veronica was to terrify her beyond measure, so that she remained mute and trembling like an aspen.

"You do not answer me, cousin," continued Bernardo, in a low, soft tone of voice unknown to him before.

"You must not love me, Bernardo," she said, at length, sadly.

"I must and will love you, cousin; you who are as bright and beautiful as the sun!"

"You must not indeed, Bernardo; you must bestow your love on some one else."

"And why should I love another, and not you?"

"Because another might be able to return your love."

"And you cannot?"

"No; I cannot."

"And why not?" asked Bernardo, returning to his usual rough voice, "why not?"

"Because it is impossible that I should love you."

"Whom *do* you love, then?"

"I do not love any one."

"I don't believe you."

"Must a young woman, then, needs have a lover?"

"She must; and when she has a lover, she

does not rest until she marries him. You must love some one; and if not me, you will love another, and I intend that you shall love me—do you understand?"

"Bernardo," said Veronica, wearied out with his impertinence, "in God's name do not detain me here with useless words or jests of gallantry, which may suit the ears of some trifling woman, but are not pleasing to me!"

Saying this, she was about moving off, when Bernardo seized her by the arm in so brutal a manner, that the poor girl gave a cry of anguish and terror.

"What right have you to treat me thus?" she demanded, indignantly.

"And what right have you to close your door in my face without listening to me?" said Bernardo, vulgarly.

"I have listened and replied to you, Bernardo, and now I am going home; for it is not proper for a young girl to stand talking to a man in the street, even though he be her cousin."

"Then let me see you at your *reja*."

"Never!"

"Give me a hope of love in the future, then, shy one—only a hope, and I will leave you!"

"You wish me to deceive you, then?"

"No, I do not wish you to deceive me, but I wish you to take time to ponder upon what I have said, before giving me a refusal as hard as the stones under our feet."

"I have well considered what I have said, and I cannot change my mind. I like to speak plainly, cousin."

"You have not considered one thing, however," said Bernardo, bitterly; "that if you despise me, I will be revenged on Juan de Silva!" and he strode away, leaving Veronica alone in the street, and as much astonished at hearing this mention of Juan de Silva, with whom she had not the slightest acquaintance, although he was her neighbor, as she had previously been at his rude declaration of love.

CHAPTER IV.

Some months had elapsed since the death of her husband, and poor Maria sat in her solitary parlor. In her pallid and wrinkled face could be seen traces of unceasing suffering and dread. Veronica was by her side, like the angels of God whom grief attracts instead of driving away, since it affords them an opportunity of exercising their mission of good-will to men.

"Aunt, what is the matter with you?" she said, with her soft, low voice, "that you have been crying all the morning?"

"My child, your cousin went out yesterday morning, and has not returned yet! I cannot help fearing that some evil has befallen him."

"Why, aunt, he often stays away from home two or three days, you know; he has probably gone to Puerto to see the bull-fight."

"If he went to Puerto, he should have returned before this, for the bull-fight came off yesterday."

At this moment, Maria's sister, the mother of Veronica, entered the room, crying out, "Maria, there is a fight in the street, and your son is one of the combatants."

Maria rose precipitately, and, without even throwing a shawl over her head, rushed into the street and in the direction indicated, followed by her sister and Veronica.

When they reached the place where the fight was going on, Maria—this woman so retiring and timid in her nature—threw herself between two men, who, with faces livid with anger and eyes flashing fire, brandished razors in their right hands, and were wrapping their *mantas* about their left arms, in readiness for another encounter.

"Son, son!" she cried, throwing her arms about Bernardo, "what are you about to do?"

The mother of the other combatant, who proved to be Juan de Silva, had also arrived with a sister, and they each held Juan by an arm; but without it being necessary to use much force, because at this instant his eyes closed, the razor fell from his grasp, and he fell senseless to the ground.

"Make your escape, Bernardo," said one of his acquaintances. "The police have been sent for."

Bernardo, who was bleeding from a wound in his side, now started for home, leaning on his mother, whose clothes were saturated with his warm blood—whose ears were shocked with the obscene blasphemies and words of vengeance which fell from his lips on perceiving himself (as he supposed) mortally wounded. Veronica assisted in supporting his faltering steps, while his aunt compressed his waist-belt, in the hope of stopping or at least lessening the hemorrhage.

So they proceeded alone and without aid; for the men who had witnessed the fight had all fled upon seeing Juan de Silva fall, with that profound fear which exists among all classes in Spain of being cited as a witness in a criminal case.

No one spoke; for debility had, at length, sealed Bernardo's lips, while the grief of the women was too great for words. In this way they reached home; and now what a group these three sisters of charity (for in sorrow and suffering all women are such) formed about the bed on which they had placed that man of frightful aspect, who, white as the wall from loss of blood, with mouth half opened and eyes glazed and wandering, lay there senseless and immovable! Staining their pure and innocent hands in the blood which sin and passion had caused to flow, Maria and her sister bound up the wound of the delinquent, and wiped the sweat of anguish from his brow; while Veronica flew to the house of Dr. Gonzales, the principal surgeon of the town, with whom she soon returned to take her place by the bedside of her cousin.

The doctor declared the wound serious, but not mortal, and, after dressing it, took his leave. Then Maria, no longer able to contain herself, hid her face in her hands and sobbed aloud—"My son, my son! He has come to a bad end at last, as his father predicted."

"Aunt, don't afflict yourself as one without hope, nor look at the clouds without remembering the rainbow. Who knows but God has chosen this method of reforming Bernardo? Don't we see in the lives of the saints how many of them God called to Himself through sickness, shipwrecks, and other calamities, which place men face to face with eternity? Bernardo will get well, aunt, so the doctor assures us, and God may be pleased, in His infinite mercy, to heal body and soul at the same time."

"Veronica, my child, God will reward you for the balsam which your words of consolation have poured into my soul. You do not know, darling, what it is to feel a pang for which there is no alleviation."

"There cannot be such, aunt," replied Veronica; "for God offers consolation to all who fervently ask it; and the greatest of all lies in knowing that our afflictions are received by His Majesty as offerings when presented as such. Who, then, in order to have an offering to present to the Lord which may be pleasing to Him, would not wish to suffer as Saint Theresa ardently desired to suffer?"

"Holy Mother!" cried Maria, ecstatically, "if I have to witness my son's, as I witnessed his father's death, God's holy will be done! But thou, afflicted Mother, grant me thy last consolation, and through thy blessed intercession let it happen that as had the father, so may the son have, a Christian death—a Christian burial!"

CHAPTER V.

AFTER the lapse of three days, which Maria had passed by the bedside of her son, between the agony of fear and the consolation of hope, without closing her eyes except to weep, nor opening her lips but to pray, the patient came out of his lethargy and gave signs of life; that is to say, he sighed and made a slight movement, and then in a faint whisper uttered some words which his mother, leaning over him, made out to be—

> "And then came out Veronica,
>   A maid of humble race;
> Who thrice knelt down upon the ground,
>   And kissed the sacred place;
> And then with snowy handkerchief—"

"The verses you were in the habit of reciting when a child, Veronica," exclaimed Maria.

"Go back, my son, go back to the days of your innocence. Do not be discouraged, and believe it impossible. Repentance and reformation open to us a new life; and the father seats the penitent prodigal at the head of his table. So God, Himself made man, has told us, promising a pardon to all those who with true repentance turn unto Him, for—

'Those who, weeping and kneeling, humbly pray,
God accepts always—never drives away.'"

"Who speaks to me of God?" said Bernardo, opening his eyes and fixing them on Maria. "My mother! Who could it be but my mother?"

"It is my duty, son of my soul."

"Do not call me son!" exclaimed Bernardo.

"And why not, ungrateful child?"

"Because I do not deserve to be called so."

Saying these words, the patient began to weep bitterly.

"Debility!" said the surgeon, who entered at this instant.

"God, who through the intercession of His

Holy Mother, the special advocate of all mothers, touches his heart," exclaimed Maria, shedding tears of joy.

"A little wine," commanded the doctor.

"No, no," cried Bernardo. "I will not touch another drop of it as long as I live."

Maria crossed her hands with exalted gratitude, and raising her eyes to heaven, "Antonio," she cried, "from the mansions of the just bless thy child, and recall the terrible prediction which thy fears drew from thee on the bed of death!"

"Hold there," said the surgeon, smiling. "Not to drink wine when you have recovered your health, is all very well; but you must take this little now as a medicine. Let him have next a cup of broth, and see that he neither speaks to any one nor is spoken to. Did I not tell you, Aunt Maria," he added, as he took his leave, "did I not tell you he would get well? Ill-weeds never die."

Some days after this, Bernardo was in full convalescence.

"And so my son," said his mother to him one morning, "you will never drink liquor again?"

"Never! for liquor has been the evil genius who incited me to commit all the wicked deeds I have been guilty of since I became a man."

"I know it, my child; for you are not naturally wicked. I trusted to the Virgin, who has so much influence with Him who is all-powerful. And that you may feel full confidence in the forgiveness of God, if you truly repent, I will narrate to you a case in point.

"There was once a poor widow, who had an only son, who was one of the most profligate of men. The poor mother was worn out with grief, and did not eat a morsel of bread that was not watered with her tears; but she prayed without ceasing to the Virgin to have pity upon her child, and bring him back to the fold of the Good Shepherd. In the mean time, the sinner persevered in his evil courses, adding crime to crime, until finally he was obliged to fly from the village in which he lived. As he wandered from place to place, harassed continually by the officers of justice, it happened that one day, overcome with heat and fatigue, he entered a small chapel, which stood quite alone in a desert spot. He leaned against a pillar, and cast his eyes toward the altar, upon which was a beautiful image of Our Lady with the Child. The wicked man looked at her, withdrew his eyes, and again gazed upon her. Upon seeing her with the Child in her arms, he remembered his mother, and bitter anguish filled his heart. He wished to shake it off, and could not; he wished to go, and remained, because that Lady looked at him with so much sweetness and compassion that she seemed to beg him to stay, until, overcome by his emotions, with tears streaming from his eyes, he fell to the ground, crying out, 'Mercy, my Mother, mercy!'

"On seeing him prostrate and weeping, the Virgin said to the Child: 'My Son, pardon this repentant sinner.' But Jesus answered: 'It cannot be; his evil deeds outweigh all clemency.'

"The sinner, hearing this, beat his breast, and, sobbing aloud, exclaimed: 'Mother of the Forsaken, behold me forsaken by God and man for my wickedness. Do not thou desert me also, Refuge of Sinners, for so my mother taught me to call you; that mother who trusted so devoutly to thy intercession.'

"'Son,' said the Virgin again, 'for his mother's sake, who was so faithful a worshipper of mine, by his tears, and by the precious blood which you shed to redeem sinners, pardon this unhappy man.'

"The wretched sinner now beat his forehead against the stones of the pavement, and cried, 'My Mother, my Mother! must I be condemned? Will the gates of heaven be eternally closed against one who at last opens his eyes to the light and detests his faults?'

"'Son,' sighed the Virgin, 'how long have you been deaf to the voice of penitence? What has this sinner done more than others?'

"'He has emancipated himself, in his pride, from his God.'

"'Now he humbles himself before Him, and, prostrate, adores Him.'

"'He has profaned my temple.'

"'Now he consecrates and purifies it with his tears.'

"'He has, by his bad example, led many astray.'

"'Now he will edify many by his conversion.'

"'His crimes are legion.'

"'So are his tears of contrition.'

"And descending from the altar, the Lady placed her Son upon it, kneeled before Him and said: 'Son, here at thy feet, I implore thee to pardon this sinner.'

"What are you doing, what are you doing, my mother?' cried the Child, raising the Lady. 'Who ever beheld a mother kneeling before the son whom she had brought into the world? Rise, and let him be pardoned who trusted so implicitly in your intercession.'

"Upon hearing this merciful sentence, the sinner raised his eyes, and, extending his arms toward the Saviour, gave a shout of jubilee, and expired.

"So you see, son," added Maria, "that in no case is hope proscribed nor mercy denied to the contrite penitent."

"What a blessing it is to have a good mother!" said Bernardo.

"And this we all have in the most Holy Virgin," answered Maria.

A few days after this, and as he was convalescing, body and soul, Bernardo was seized by the authorities and sent to jail—since, although Juan de Silva had not died, Bernardo was proved to have been the aggressor in the contest.

We will not attempt to describe the grief of the unhappy mother.

CHAPTER VI.

A YEAR had passed, and the patient and submissive Maria lay upon her bed, listening to Veronica, who was reading to her a letter, written on fine paper and in a handsome hand. In the pallid face of that woman, a living image of suffering, there appeared a soft expression of happiness which, though it could not light her almost-darkened eyes, played in a sweet smile about her lips.

"There is always something, my child," said the poor mother, "to thank God for, who never wounds with both hands. The stab which my son gave Juan de Silva did not prove mortal, and so my poor son has not a murder upon his conscience. He was condemned for four years to the penitentiary at Melilla, and a charitable man has had his place of imprisonment changed to the Trocadero, where the convicts are working; so we can often go to see him. He is in despair at the idea of being a prisoner for four years, and threatens to make his escape whenever an opportunity offers, although I do my best to convince him that he should bear his sentence with patience and resignation. And now see how this great lady, Doña Laura de Guzman—who came here last summer to bathe in the ocean and learned of my misfortunes through your mother, who washed for her—see with what goodness and charity she has taken the trouble to send me a letter in her own handwriting, to say that the regent promised to release Bernardo shortly, on learning from her that I was sick and almost blind, with this only son for my protection!"

"God grant that he may be such!" sighed Veronica.

"And why is it," continued the excellent old woman, "that ill-natured poor people are continually murmuring at the rich, for no other reason, that I can see, than that they *are* rich? I am of the opinion, Veronica, that if these grumblers were wealthy, they would treat us poor people with much more haughtiness and much less charity than we now receive. May God bless the charitable lady who has befriended me, and grant that her life may be long and happy, and her death peaceful and holy!"

"You may well be grateful to her," said Veronica, "for she has obtained a great favor for you."

"It is very true," answered Maria; "but is it not sufficient punishment for his offence, my child, to have had irons on his feet for a whole year—those feet which I have so often kissed when he was a child—so often wrapped in my apron! Oh, why do not children remain always small in their bodies and angels in their souls? But I must not waste time in talking. I wish to go myself to carry this letter of glad tidings to my boy."

"Aunt," exclaimed Veronica, "what are you thinking of, as ill as you are, to talk of walking such a distance? It is impossible!"

"I *must* go, my darling. Don't you know that happiness gives strength? But if you do not wish me to walk there, run with all speed to the house of the boatman Miguel Santos, and ask him if he will, for charity's sake, take me to the Trocadero in his launch."

Maria now got up and dressed, while Veronica ran to see the boatman, with whom she soon returned, in order that they might both together carry her aunt to the boat.

"I would not have gone afloat to-day for any one but you, Aunt Maria," said Miguel, "for last night I was fishing by torchlight, and I feel sleepy this morning and wished to rest? and besides, the last night was the most terrible of my life. God grant I may never pass such another!"

"What could have happened to you; for the night was as serene and tranquil as my soul is at this moment, thanks to God and to Doña Laura de Guzman!" said Maria.

"You must know," replied the boatman "that as I was fishing off the Trocadero, I heard about midnight, coming frem the centre of the marshes, a sound so piteous that it fairly froze the blood in my veins. I could not imagine what it was—whether the howling of a dog, the cry of a human being, or the lamentation of a lost soul; for the distance whence it came was great, and if it reached my ears it was only because the night was as still as death.

"All who are acquainted with Miguel Santos well know that he is not one of those who turn their backs when danger threatens, nor is he disturbed by a slight thing, but I am not ashamed to confess that in this instance my hair stood on end, and that I crossed myself like a Christian; for neither am I a man who fears not God nor the devil. As soon as I had composed myself somewhat, I listened attentively, to see if I could ascertain whence the sound came, and what it really was. And now came the worst; for I comprehended, by degrees, that it was the voice of a human being in distress—always proceeding from the same spot, and in the same piteous tone, like the *bell of agony*. I asked myself if it could possibly be the signal of some smuggler—but no; I could not deceive myself: it was a wail, such as I trust His Divine Majesty will never permit me to hear again. Each time that I heard it, I shook as if I had an ague-fit! I could neither fish nor sit still, nor do any thing, in fact, but recommend that unfortunate being to the clemency of God, because, as I have already told you, the night was as dark as the conscience of Judas, and the voice came from the marshes among which only those who know every foot of them can walk, even by day, for when one steps into a quicksand—from God comes the remedy!"

The fisherman made a pause, and raised his hair from his forehead, as if it burnt him.

"But Miguel," said Maria, profoundly interested in his narration, "you ascertained what it was before you left there?"

"Yes, indeed," answered Santos, "for the dawn with its light came to confirm what my heart had long foreboded. The cries of the unfortunate, growing fainter and fainter, as the night wore away, had long since ceased altogether; but as I had well noted the direction whence they came, I landed, and, as I best could, made my way through the marshes, which I know as well as I know the palms of my hands, until I came to a spot where two hands sticking out, like the cross over a grave, showed that a man had been buried alive there. All night had this burial been taking place, and I, O God! so near, and unable to assist the sufferer!"

"Jesus, Jesus!" exclaimed at the same instant Veronica and her aunt, "who could this unhappy man have been?"

"It could only have been one of the prisoners trying to make his escape from the Trocadero."

At this moment an officer of justice entered. "I come," said he, roughly, "to search the house."

"Why so," cried Maria, in an agonized tone—"why so, sir?"

"Because your son made his escape from the fort last night."

Maria gave a sharp cry, and extended her hands before her, as if to drive away some frightful apparition.

"What is the matter with her?" asked the officer. "What does this mean?"

"It means," replied Miguel, "that he who fled missed the path, stepped into a quicksand and was buried alive!"

"Do you know this to be a fact?"

"I was, I may say, present, without having it in my power to render assistance to the poor fellow," responded Miguel, sorrowfully. "Go to the swamp, and unless the earth has already swallowed them, you will see two hands which say, 'Here lies a Christian.'"

The officer departed.

"My son, my son!" now shrieked Maria, "son of my life, son of my soul! How he must have suffered! Oh, my God, my God! To die without aid human or divine, while I, who brought thee forth, slept! Thy father well said—'*He will come to a bad end!*' Alas for me, unhappy mother!—alas for thee, oh, unfortunate and miserable son! God has forsaken us both!"

"Aunt, aunt," exclaimed the weeping Veronica, "God never forsakes any one."

"Let Him then aid me now!" cried Maria, trembling from head to foot. "Let Him aid me now!"

"Say first, as a submissive child," sobbed Veronica, "*Thy will be done.*"

"Thy will be done!" repeated the despairing but truly religious woman, making the sign of the cross with her trembling fingers; "and if, like the child of my soul, I too must die without consolation—*Thy will be done! Thy will be done!*"

"One consolation still remains to you," said Miguel, gravely.

"For me? There can be none for me now," groaned Maria.

"And would not the certainty that your son died a Christian be such?"

"Ah! if I had but this; if the Holy Virgin had heard the petition of my whole life since I became a mother!"

"Your prayer was granted."

"My prayer was granted!" murmured Maria, her voice choking with emotion, "who can assure me of this?"

"I, who know his last thought," responded the boatman, solemnly—"I, who beheld the cross raised above his grave—the cross which he had formed with his fingers, to attest that he died as a Christian; that is, repenting of his sins, believing, loving, and hoping in God."

The fervent Christian dropped on her knees, crossed her hands, and exclaimed: "My son died a Christian! Glory be to God, and blessed be thou, Mother of Mercy! Glory, glory, glory!"

Exhausted nature could bear no more. The poor mother fell forward, with her face to the earth. When they raised her, life was extinct.

On the day of her burial, the place pointed out by the fisherman as the grave of Bernardo was consecrated, and the funeral service read over it, so that Maria's prayer—" As had the father, so may the son have a Christian death, a Christian burial "—was fully answered by the Virgin.

THE END.

THE
Catholic Publication Society's
BOOKS.

Abridgment of the Christian Doctrine. By the Right Rev. Bishop Hay. 32mo, cloth, ... $0 25

An Amicable Discussion on the Church of England, and on the Reformation in General. Dedicated to the Clergy of every Protestant Communion, and reduced into the form of letters by the Right Rev. J. F. M. Trevern, D.D., Bishop of Strasbourg. Translated by the Rev. Wm. Richmond. 1 vol. 12mo, 580 pp., ... $2 00

An Illustrated History of Ireland, from the Earliest Period to the Present Time; with several first-class full-page Engravings of Historical Scenes, designed by Henry Doyle, and engraved by George Hanlon and George Pearson; together with upwards of 100 woodcuts, by eminent artists, illustrating Antiquities, Scenery, and Sites of Remarkable Events; and three large maps, one of Ireland and the others of Family Homes, Statistics, etc. 1 vol. 8vo, nearly 700 pp. New and enlarged edition. Extra cloth, $5 00; half calf, ... $7 00

Anima Divota; or, Devout Soul. Translated from the Italian of Very Rev. J. B. Pagani, Provincial of the Order of Charity in England. 24mo, cloth, $0 60

Anne Severin. By the Author of "A Sister's Story." 1 vol. 12mo, cloth, $1 50; cloth, gilt, ... $2 00

Apologia pro Vita Sua: Being a Reply to a Pamphlet entitled "What, then, does Dr. Newman Mean?" By John Henry Newman, D.D. New edition. 1 vol. 12mo, ... $2 00

A Sister's Story. By Mrs. Augustus Craven. Translated from the French by Emily Bowles. 1 vol. crown 8vo, pp. 558. Cloth, extra, $2 50; vellum cloth, gilt, ... $3 00

Aspirations of Nature. By Rev. I. T. Hecker. 4th edition, revised, cloth, extra, ... $1 50

Beauties of Sir Thomas More. A Selection from his Works, as well in prose as in verse. A sequel to "Life and Times of More." By W. J. Walter. 18mo, cloth, ... $1 25

Bona Mors. A Pious Association of the Devout Servants of our Lord Jesus Christ dying on the Cross in order to obtain a Good Death. 24mo, cloth, $0 25

Catechism of Council of Trent. 8vo, ... $2 00

Catholic Christian Instructed. By the Right Rev. Dr. Challoner. 24mo, flexible cloth, $0 25; extra cloth, ... $0 40

List of Books.

The Same. 12mo, large type, flexible cloth, $0 40; extra cloth, . . $0 75

Catholic Manual; containing a Selection of Prayers and Devotional Exercises. 18mo, embossed, $1 00; roan, 2 plates, $1 50; roan, gilt edge, 4 plates, $1 75; turkey morocco, super extra, 8 plates, . . . $3 00

Christian's Guide to Heaven. 32mo, cloth, $0 50; roan, 4 engravings, $0 60 roan, gilt edge, 4 engravings, $1 00; turkey, super extra, 6 engravings, $2 25

Christine and Other Poems. By George H. Miles. Illustrated, . $2 00

Compendious Abstract of the History of the Church of Christ. By Rev. Wm. Gahan. 12mo, ... $1 00

Confidence in the Mercy of God. By the Right Rev. Joseph Languet. 18mo, cloth, ... $0 50

Cradle Lands: Egypt, Palestine, etc. By Lady Herbert. 1 vol. 12mo, vellum cloth, $2 00; cloth, gilt, $2 50; half calf, $4 00; full calf, red edges, . $6 00

Daily Companion; containing a Selection of Prayers and Devotional Exercises for the Use of Children. Embellished with 36 very neat illustrative engravings. 32mo, cloth, $0 25; roan, ... $0 60

Defence of Catholic Principles. By the Rev. D. A. Gallitzin. 4th edition, 18mo, cloth, ... $0 60

Devout Communicant. By the Rev. P. Baker. New edition, 24mo, cloth, $0 60; roan, $1 25; roan, gilt edges, $1 75; turkey morocco, super extra, $3 00

Douay Bible. 12mo, suitable for Missionaries. Embellished, . . $1 50

Douay Testament. A beautiful pocket edition. 32mo, cloth, $0 45; roan, embossed, $0 60; roan, embossed, gilt edges, $1 00; tuck, gilt edges, $1 25; fine edition, roan, $1 00; fine edition, roan, gilt edge, $1 50; fine edition, turkey morocco, super extra, ... $2 25

Douay Testament. 12mo, large type, embellished, ... $0 75

Epistle of Jesus Christ to the Faithful Soul, ... $1 00

Eugenie de Guerin, Journal of, ... $2 00

Eugenie de Guerin, Letters of, ... $2 00

Exposition of the Doctrine of the Catholic Church in Matters of Controversy. By the Right Rev. J. B. Bossuet. A new edition, with copious notes, by Rev. J. Fletcher, D.D. 18mo, $0 60; another edition, without notes, 32mo, cloth, ... $0 25

Father Rowland. A North American Tale. 18mo, cloth, . . $0 60

Following of Christ. In four books. By Thomas à Kempis, With Reflections at the conclusion of each Chapter. 18mo, cloth, $0 75; roan, plates, $1 50; roan, gilt edge, plates, $1 75; turkey morocco, super extra, . . $3 00

The Same. Pocket edition, without the Reflections, 32mo, cloth, $0 25; roan, $0 60; roan, gilt edge, $1 00; turkey morocco, super extra, . . $2 25

Garden of the Soul; or, A Manual of Spiritual Exercises and Instructions for Christians, who, living in the world, aspire to devotion. By Right Rev. Dr. Challoner. 24mo, arabesque, $0 50; roan, 2 plates, $0 75; roan, gilt edges, 4 plates, $1 00; turkey, super extra, 8 plates, ... $2 50

Genevieve: A Tale of Antiquity, showing the Wonderful Ways of Providence in the Protection of Innocence. From the German of Schmid. 18mo, cloth $0 60

Glimpses of Pleasant Homes. By the Author of "The Life of Mother McCauley." Illustrated with four full-page illustrations. 1 vol. 12mo, cloth, extra, $1 50; cloth, gilt, ... $2 00

Gropings after Truth: A Life-Journey from New-England Congregationalism to the One Catholic Apostolic Church. By Joshua Huntington. 1 vol. vellum cloth, ... $0 75

Grounds of the Catholic Doctrine, contained in the Profession of Faith published by Pope Pius IV. 32mo, cloth, ... $0 20

Historical Catechism. By M. l'Abbé Fleury. Parts I. and II., revised by Right Rev. Bishop Cheverus. 18mo, paper cover, $0 12; complete, in four parts, 18mo, ... $0 60

History of England, for the Use of Schools, to the end of the Reign of George IV. By W. F. Mylius. 12mo, ... $1 00

History of the Church from its Establishment to the Reformation. By Rev. C. C. Pise. 5 vols. 8vo, $7 50; another edition, 5 vols. 12mo, cloth, $5 00

History of the Old and New Testaments. By J. Reeve. 8vo, half-bound, roan, ... $1 00

Hornihold. The Commandments and Sacraments Explained in Fifty-two Discourses. By the Right Rev. Dr. Hornihold, author of "Real Principles of Catholics." 12mo, cloth, ... $2 00

Home of the Lost Child. 18mo, cloth, ... $0 60

Homilies on the Book of Tobias; or, A Familiar Explanation of the Practical Duties of Domestic Life. By Rev. T. Martyn. 12mo, cloth, $0 75

Hours of the Passion; or, Pathetic Reflections on the Sufferings and Death of our Blessed Redeemer. By St. Liguori. New edition, translated by Right Rev. W. Walsh, late Bishop of Halifax. 18mo, cloth, . . $0 60

Imitation of the Blessed Virgin. In four books. 18mo, cloth, . $0 60

Impressions of Spain. By Lady Herbert. 1 vol. 12mo. 15 illustrations. Cloth, extra, $2 00; cloth, gilt, $2 50; half morocco, or calf, $4 00; full calf, $6 00

In Heaven we know Our Own, ... $0 60

Interior Christian. In eight books, with a supplement; extracted from the writings of M. Bernier de Louvigny. 18mo, cloth, . . . $0 60

Introduction to a Devout Life. From the French of St. Francis of Sales. 18mo, cloth, ... $0 75

Irish Odes and Other Poems. By Aubrey de Vere. 1 vol. 12mo, toned paper, $2 00; cloth, gilt, ... $2 50

Key of Paradise, opening the Gate to Eternal Salvation. 18mo, arabesque, $1 00; roan, 2 plates, $1 50; roan, gilt edge, 4 plates, $1 75; turkey morocco, super extra, 8 plates, ... $3 00

Lenten Monitor; or, Moral Reflections and Devout Aspirations on the Gospel. By Rev. P. Baker, O.S.F. 24mo, cloth, New edition, $0 60

Letters to a Prebendary. Being an Answer to "Reflections on Popery," by Rev. J. Sturgis, LL.D. By Right Rev. J. Milner, D.D. 24mo, cloth, $0 60

Letters to a Protestant Friend on the Holy Scriptures. By Rev. D. A. Gallitzin. 18mo, cloth, ... $0 60

Life and Times of Sir Thomas More, Illustrated from his Own Writings. By W. J. Walter. With a portrait and autograph of More. 18mo, cloth, $0 25

Life of St. Catharine of Sienna, ... $1 75

Life of St. Vincent de Paul. 32mo, cloth, ... $0 45

Little Treatise on the Little Virtues. Written originally in Italian, by Father Roberti, of the Society of Jesus. To which are added, "A Letter on

List of Books.

Fervor," by Father Vallois, and "Maxims," from an unpublished manuscript of J. B. Walsh, late Bishop of Halifax. New edition, 18mo, cloth, $0 60

May Carols, and Hymns and Poems. By Aubrey de Vere. Blue and gold, ... $1 25

Memorial of a Christian Life. By Rev. Lewis de Granada. Revised edition. 18mo, cloth, ... $0 75

Memorials of those who Suffered for the Catholic Faith in Ireland during the Sixteenth, Seventeenth, and Eighteenth Centuries. Collected and edited by Myles O'Reilly, B.A., LL.D. 1 vol. crown 8vo, vellum cloth, $2 50; cloth, gilt, $3 00; half calf, . . . $4 50

Month of Mary, containing a Series of Meditations, etc., in honor of the B.V.M. Arranged for each day of the month. 32mo, cloth, . . $0 40

Nellie Netterville; or, One of the Transplanted. A Tale of the Times of Cromwell in Ireland. 1 vol. 12mo, cloth, extra, $1 50; cloth, gilt, $2 00

Net for the Fishers of Men, ... $0 06

Nouet. Meditations on the Life and Passion of our Lord Jesus Christ for every Day in the Year. By Rev. J. Nouet, S. J. To which are added, "Meditations on the Sacred Heart of Jesus Christ," being those taken from a Nouvena in preparation for the Feast of the same. By Father C. Borgo, S. J. 1 vol. 12mo, 880 pp., ... $2 50

Office of the Holy Week, according to the Roman Missal and Breviary, in Latin and English. 18mo, cloth, $0 75; roan, 1 plate, $1 50; roan, gilt edge, 2 plates, $2 00; turkey morocco, super extra, 4 plates, . . $3 50

O'Kane. Notes on the Rubrics of the Roman Ritual. 1 vol. 12mo, . $4 00

Oratory of the Faithful Soul; or, Devotions to the Most Holy Sacrament and to our Blessed Lady. Translated from the works of Ven. Abbot Blosius. By Robert Aston Coffin. 18mo, cloth, ... $0 50

Packets of Scripture Illustrations. Containing 50 engravings of subjects from the Old and New Testaments, after original designs by Elster. Loose packages of 50, ... $0 75

Path to Paradise. A Selection of Prayers and Devotions for Catholics. 48mo, cloth, $0 20; roan, $0 40; roan, gilt, $0 60; turkey morocco, sup. extra, 4 engravings, ... $1 25

Pious Guide to Prayer and Devotion. Containing various Practices of Piety, calculated to Answer the Demands of the Devout Members of the Catholic Church. 18mo, arabesque, $1 00; roan, 2 plates, $1 50; roan, gilt edge, 4 plates, $1 75; turkey morocco, super extra, 8 plates, $3 00; various styles in velvet and turkey morocco, with clasps and ornaments, from $4 50 to $10 00. A new and beautiful edition, containing the same as the above large edition, 24mo, arabesque, $0 60; roan, 2 plates, $1 00; roan, gilt edge, 4 plates, $1 50; turkey morocco, super extra, 8 plates, . . $2 50

Poor Man's Catechism; or, The Christian Doctrine Explained, with Short Admonitions. By John Mannock, O.S.B. 24mo, cloth, . . $0 50

Poor Man's Manual of Devotion; or, Devout Christian's Daily Companion. To which is added, "Daily Devotion; or, Profitable Manner of Hearing Mass." 24mo, arabesque, $0 50; roan, $0 80; roan, gilt edge, $1 50; turkey, super extra, ... $2 50

Poor Man's Controversy. By J. Mannock, Author of "Poor Man's Catechism." 18mo, cloth, ... $0 50

Practical Discourses on the Perfections and Works of God, and the Divinity and Works of Jesus Christ. By the Rev. J. Reeve. 8vo, cloth, . $2 00

Problems of the Age, with Studies in St. Augustine on Kindred Topics. By Rev. Augustine F. Hewit. 1 vol. 12mo, cloth, extra, . . $2 00

Questions of the Soul. By Rev. I. T. Hecker. New edition, $1 50; cloth, gilt, ... $2 00

Reason and Revelation. Lectures delivered in St. Ann's Church, New York, during Advent, 1867. By Rev. T. S. Preston. 1 vol. 12mo, . $1 50

Sacred Heart of Jesus and the Sacred Heart of Mary. Translated from the Italian of Father Lanzi, Author of "History of Painting," etc., with an Introduction by Rev. C. B. Meehan. 24mo, cloth, ... $0 60

St. Columba, Apostle of Caledonia. By the Count de Montalembert. 1 vol. 12mo, toned paper, $1 25; cloth, gilt, ... $1 75

Sermons of the Paulist Fathers for the Years 1865 and 1866, $1 50

Sermons of the Paulist Fathers for the Year 1864. New edition, $1 50

Short Treatise on Prayer, adapted to all Classes of Christians. By St. Alphonsus Liguori. New edition, 24mo, cloth, ... $0 40

Spirit of St. Alphonsus de Liguori. A Selection from his shorter Spiritual Treatises. Translated by the Rev. J. Jones. 24mo, cloth, . . $0 60

Spiritual Combat. To which is added, "The Peace of the Soul and the Happiness of the Heart which Dies to Itself in Order to Live to God." 32mo, ... $0 40

Spiritual Consoler; or, Instructions to Enlighten Pious Souls in their Doubts, etc. By Father Quadrupani. 18mo, ... $0 50

Spiritual Director of Devout and Religious Souls. By St. Francis de Sales, ... $0 50

Stories on the Seven Virtues. By Agnes M. Stewart, Authoress of "Festival of the Rosary." 18mo, cloth, ... $0 60

Symbolism; or, Exposition of the Doctrinal Differences between Catholics and Protestants, as evidenced by their Symbolical Writings. By John A. Mochler, D.D. Translated from the German, with a Memoir of the Author, preceded by an Historical Sketch of the State of Protestantism and Catholicism in Germany for the last Hundred Years, by J. B. Robertson, Esq., $4 00

Tales from the Diary of a Sister of Mercy. By C. M. Brame. 1 vol. 12mo, cloth, extra, $1 50; cloth, gilt, ... $2 00

The Clergy and the Pulpit, in their Relations to the People. By M. l'Abbé Isidore Mullois, Chaplain to Napoleon III. 1 vol. 12mo, extra cloth, ... $1 50

The Comedy of Convocation in the English Church. In Two Scenes. Edited by Archdeacon Chasuble, D.D., and dedicated to the Pan-Anglican Synod. 8vo, pamphlet. Paper, $0 75; bound in cloth, . . . $1 00

The Holy Communion; Its Philosophy, Theology, and Practice. By John Bernard Dalgairns, Priest of the Oratory of Saint Philip Neri. 1 vol. 12mo, ... $2 00

The Illustrated Catholic Sunday-School Library. 1st Series. 12 vols. handsomely bound, and put up in a box. Cloth, extra, $6 00; cloth, gilt, $7 50

The Illustrated Catholic Sunday-School Library. 2d Series. 12 vols handsomely bound in cloth, put up in a box. Cloth, extra, $6 00; cloth gilt, ... $7 50

The Illustrated Catholic Sunday-School Library. 3d Series. 12 vols. in box. Cloth, extra, $6 00; gilt, ... $7 50

The Inner Life of the Very Rev. Pere Lacordaire, of the Order of Preachers. Translated from the French of the Rev. Pere Chocarne, O. P

List of Books.

By a Father of the same Order; with Preface by Father Aylward, Prior Provincial of England. 1 vol. 12mo, toned paper, ... $3 00

The Life and Sermons of the Rev. Francis A. Baker, Priest of the Congregation of St. Paul. Edited by Rev. A. F. Hewit. 1 vol. crown 8vo, pp. 504. $2 50; half calf, ... $4 00

The Life of Father Ravignan, S. J. By Father Ponlevoy, S. J. 1 vol. crown 8vo, toned paper, ... $4 00

The People's Pictorial Lives of the Saints, Scriptural and Historical. Abridged, for the most part, from those of the late Rev. Alban Butler. These are got up expressly for Sunday-school presents. In packets of 12 each. One packet now ready, containing the lives of twelve different saints. Per packet, ... $0 25

The See of St. Peter. The Rock of the Church, the Source of Jurisdiction, and Centre of Unity. By Thomas William Allies, M.A. 1 vol. 16mo, . $0 75

The Two Schools. A Moral Tale. By Mrs. Hughs. 12mo, cloth, . $0 75

The Works of the Most Rev. John Hughes, D.D., First Archbishop of New York, containing Biography, Sermons, Letters, Lectures, Speeches, etc. Carefully compiled from the best sources, and edited by Lawrence Kehoe. This important work makes 2 large vols. of nearly 1,500 pp. 8vo. Cloth, $6 00; half calf, extra, ... $12 00

Think Well On't; or, The Great Truths of the Christian Religion for Every Day in the Month. By Right Rev. R. Challoner. 32mo, cloth, . $0 25

Three Phases of Christian Love : The Mother, the Maiden, and the Religious. By Lady Herbert. 1 vol. 12mo, vellum cloth, $1 50; gilt, $2 00

Triumph of Religion; or, A Choice Selection of Edifying Narratives. 18mo, cloth, ... $0 60

True Piety; or, The Day Well Spent. A Manual of Fervent Prayers, Pious Reflections, and Solid Instructions for the Members of the Catholic Church. 18mo, arabesque, $1 00; roan, 2 plates, $1 50; roan, gilt edge, 4 plates, $1 75; turkey morocco, super extra, 8 plates, . . . $3 00

Visits to the Blessed Sacrament and to the Blessed Virgin for Every Day in the Month. By St. Alphonsus Liguori. 24mo, cloth. New edition, ... $0 75

Way of Salvation. Meditations for Every Day in the Year. By St. Alphonsus Liguori. 24mo, cloth, ... $0 75

Why Men do not Believe; or, The Principal Causes of Infidelity. Translated from the French of Mgr. Laforet. Cloth, ... $1 00

Any Book on this List sent by mail, post-paid, on receipt of the advertised price.

THE CATHOLIC PUBLICATION SOCIETY,

LAWRENCE KEHOE, General Agent,

9 Warren St., New York.

CHEAP BOOKS IN PAPER COVERS.

THE
CATHOLIC PUBLICATION SOCIETY

HAS JUST ISSUED

"PEOPLE'S EDITIONS"

Of the following Excellent Books, in Paper Covers.

I. BOOKS OF DOCTRINE AND CONTROVERSY.

1. *The Catholic Christian Instructed.* By Bishop Challoner. 20 cents.
2. *The Catholic Christian Instructed.* (Large type.) 25 cents.
3. *Bossuet's Exposition of the Doctrines of the Catholic Church on Matters of Controversy.* With Notes. Large Edition. 25 cents.
4. *Bossuet's Exposition of the Doctrines of the Catholic Church on Matters of Controversy.* Without Notes. Small Edition. 20 cents.
5. *The Poor Man's Catechism; or, The Christian Doctrine Explained.* 25 cents.
6. *The Poor Man's Controversy.* 25 cents.
7. *Gallitzin's Defence of Catholic Principles.* 25 cents.
8. *Gallitzen on the Holy Scriptures.* 25 cents.

II. BOOKS OF BIOGRAPHY, TRAVELS, INSTRUCTION, AND AMUSEMENT.

1. *Memorials of those who Suffered for the Faith* in Ireland in the Sixteenth, Seventeenth, and Eighteenth Centuries. By Myles O'Reilly.
2. *A Sister's Story.* By Mrs. Augustus Craven.
3. *Apologia pro Vita Sua.* By Dr. Newman.

☞ *Single copies of the above works,* $1 *each.*

4. *The Life of the Rev. Francis A. Baker.* By Rev. A. F. Hewit.
5. *Three Phases of Christian Love.* By Lady Herbert.
6. *Lectures on Reason and Revelation.* By Rev. T. S. Preston.
7. *Aspirations of Nature.* By Rev. I. T. Hecker.
8. *Questions of the Soul.* By Rev. I. T. Hecker.
9. *Nellie Netterville.* A tale of the Cromwellian Settlement of Ireland. By Miss Caddell.
10. *Cradle Lands.* By Lady Herbert.
11. *Tales from the Diary of a Sister of Mercy.*
12. *Paulist Sermons for 1864.*
13. *Paulist Sermons for 1866.*
14. *The Clergy and the Pulpit.*

☞ *Single copies of the above works,* 50 *cents each.*

15. *The Comedy of Convocation in the English* Church.
16. *Gropings after Truth.* By Joshua Huntington.

☞ *Single copies of the above works,* 25 *cents.*

17. *The See of St. Peter.* By T. W. Allies. 40 cents.
18. *Why Men do not Believe; or, The Principal* Cause of Infidelity. By Mgr. Laforet. 30 cents.
19. *Impressions of Spain.* By Lady Herbert. 40 cents.
20. *Life and Letters of Madame Swetchine.* 60 cents.
21. *Letters of Eugenie de Guerin.* 75 cents.
22. *Journal of Eugenie de Guerin.* 75 cents.

THE CATHOLIC PUBLICATION SOCIETY,
LAWRENCE KEHOE,
General Agent, 9 Warren Street, New York.

☞ *Persons ordering the cheap edition of these books must be particular and state that fact, or otherwise the Library Edition will be sent.*

www.ingramcontent.com/pod-product-compliance
Lightning Source LLC
Chambersburg PA
CBHW030730230426
43667CB00007B/658